SECRET SOUNDS OF PONDS

Also by David Rothenberg

PROSE

Is It Painful to Think?
Hand's End
Sudden Music
Always the Mountains
Why Birds Sing
Thousand Mile Song
Survival of the Beautiful
Bug Music
Nightingales in Berlin
The Possibility of Reddish Green
From This World, Another
[with Stephen Nachmanovitch]
Whale Music

POETRY

Blue Cliff Record
Invisible Mountains

Secret Sounds of Ponds

David Rothenberg

ROOF BOOKS
New York

ISBN: 979-8-9896652-0-4
Library of Congress Control Number: 2023943692

Cover design by Deborah Thomas
Book design by David Rothenberg
Author photo by Gabriella Magnani

Set in Fournier MT and Tajawal
All images by the author unless noted.

 This book is made possible, in part, by the New York State
Council on the Arts with the support of the Office of the
Governor and the New York State Legislature.

Roof Books
are published by Segue Foundation
300 Bowery Fl. 2
New York, NY 10012
seguefoundation.com

Roof Books
are distributed by
Small Press Distribution
1341 Seventh Street
Berkeley, CA. 94710-1403
800-869-7553 or spdbooks.org

Lost Pond

Contents

Sound plunges below the surface. Sound penetrates to the heart of things....
I am always at the heart of the sounding universe.

—R. Murray Schafer, "I Have Never Seen a Sound"

Nothing, nothing, Kleist drinks it all in... To him the whole dark sparkling lake is the cluster of diamonds upon a vast, slumbering, unknown woman's body. The lime trees and the pine trees and the flowers give off the perfumes. There is a soft, scarcely perceptible sound down there; he can hear it, but he can also see it. That is something new. *He wants the intangible, the incomprehensible.*

—Robert Walser, *The Walk*

We are pattern makers, and if our patterns are beautiful and full of grace, they will be able to bring a person for whom the world has become broken and disorganized up off his knees and back to life.

—Barry Lopez, *Horizon*

Go outside and listen for what cannot be heard.

—Angela Rawlings, *The Sound of Mull*

Pond Emergence

From above, their depths seem mute. But for a long time, I had known that ponds were full of underwater sounds. While completely silent above the water, beneath the surface all kinds of rhythms and songs could be heard, if one had the right equipment.

I had a few underwater microphones that I use to listen to whales, in the deep and noisy ocean, but whenever I dipped these hydrophones in ponds, I heard nothing. What was I doing wrong? I had heard recordings full of swirling sounds infused with possibility. Why wasn't I hearing this in the ponds around me.

One day I went to the Wave Farm art park upstate, which features sonic artworks in a rural setting. The Brooklyn artist Zach Poff had made an incredible sound installation, a worn wooden raft permanently floating in a mucky pond, and this thing was continuously broadcasting all kinds of crazy underwater noises.

Later I asked him how he did it.

"Different technology," he wrote back. "Kind of like a waterproof contact mic. Picks up only what happens really close to it, as if it could touch the sounds." "Can you make me one?" I asked, and he obliged.

Then I went back out to listen. Here's what happened when I dropped it into a crystal lake near the tip of Cape Cod:

Cape Cod Long Pond
Provincetown, MA

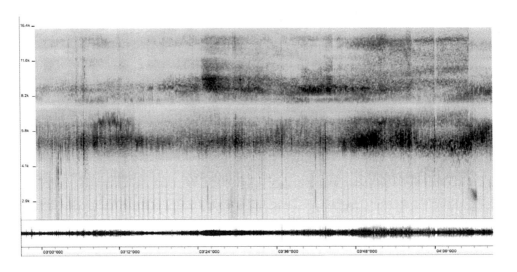

From 3:00 to 4:00, one minute total

This is what a busy pond sounds like, once you've got the right kind of hydrophone.

Keep in mind that above the water all was silent. It was only while listening deep down that this music appeared. It was midsummer, a kettle pond in Provincetown, over the first weekend in 2020 that we were actually allowed to go anywhere. The Cape was not crowded, and this pond on the bike path was ignored. We sat down and listened. Took a nap even. Midafternoon on a warm day.

I've given you a sonogram of this moment. This is an image that maps frequency against time, used by scientists, and others, to visually make sense of temporal events that we may have a hard time talking about without having a clear image of them to see.

Although these images throughout this book appear the same size, the often show different amounts of time, sometimes zoomed in, sometimes out. I'll list the number of seconds or minutes right at the bottom of each.

The dark mess toward the top of the sonogram suggests high frequency complexity, a wash of many insects stridulating, similar to crickets on land in thickets—but these are underwater.

The regular vertical lines are the pop pop bubbles of plants photosynthesizing, exchanging oxygen through the water with the air—that's where regular rhythms come from in this underwater world.

The attempt to distinguish plant from animal will be a big part of the decoding of the secret sounds of ponds. Sometimes it is easy to tell, at other times not so clear.

The QR code below is the pure original pond, nine minutes of it so you can really tune in. Later you'll hear how this piece is used as a musical background, a sonic element to inspire human play.

Take a photo of the code on your phone and it will reveal a link that plays the sound

At the end of this book all the links will be listed in one place, and I'll also tell you how to get your own hydrophone to try all this at home

Composer David Dunn heard the sounds of ponds move in and out around each other and felt an order, a logic, a beauty emerging, with no one force behind it all. This is how ecosystems work, and he was excited to discover something beautiful, musical, and unknown. He wrote this in his chapter in my *Book of Music and Nature* in 2000:

> After a couple of years of listening to these small ponds and marshes, I came to understand a pattern to their underwater sound making. The one consistent factor is how beautiful and complex these miniature sounds are. I have finally

reconciled myself to the gut feeling that these sounds are an emergent property of the pond: something that speaks as a collective voice for a mind that is beyond my grasp. I know that this is not a scientific way of thinking, but I can't help myself. Now when I see a pond, I think of the water's surface as a membrane enclosing something deep in thought.

Interspecies Internet

To go between. From one, to another. From my species to yours. The music you got, the sound out there. To find music between, music no one species could make alone. I've found it with lyrebirds, cicadas, reed warblers, and nightingales. Having heard the pond, I want to join the pond, making music no one species could make alone.

Interspecies *internet*, now that immediately suggests something else.

It's the name of the conference, a closeted gathering at MIT. Its attendees have assembled in the halls of technology's sacred temple to believe in the impossible… communication with intelligences alien to our own. Humans have dreamed of such a thing for centuries. For all the millions of hours we have spent together with animals, using, abusing, petting, and loving them, we still cannot speak with them.

It is 2019. The time of information, information for all. Data flows everywhere. Lots of it, not a little. Big data. Bigger than you know, baby.

The children get it. The son of the inventor of the Macintosh computer is talking to us from the podium. Aza Raskin—I read online that he gave his first lecture on interface design when he was eight years old. "Here's what we got," Aza says. "We fed into the machine three thousand hours of spoken French language into our program first. Then we gave it three thousand hours of spoken German. Telling the AI nothing more, it was soon able to translate fluidly between the two languages, learning from the data alone." Next slide please.

"So it is obvious what we can do next. Does anyone out there have three thousand hours of dolphin speech for us to try?" and the room breaks out into applause.

I walk out of the conference into an empty atrium in the famed Media Lab. The balcony opens out onto a sweeping view of the cities of Cambridge and Boston, where I spent so many years studying long ago. Boston University. Harvard University. Bicycling between teaching classes at each. Back then I couldn't imagine living anywhere else.

One grizzled fellow with a trimmed beard stands at the glass barrier looking out. It is Peter Gabriel. If you're too young or old to know him he is one of the great pop stars of the eighties, and a true champion of world music, even music beyond the human edge. Peter jammed with a bonobo ape named Kanzi some years back. I sent him my books, and he always wrote back. "Interesting, David," he would write. "Thank you for this." I had never met him before.

"Peter, so nice to see you here,"

He smiles. Does not try to walk away.

All those songs of my youth stream by. *In Your Eyes* I am complete. Busking on the streets of Oslo with my friend Bård, in the gray eighties before Norway found any oil. A dark song. Dark times. Here's the guy who wrote it. Wow.

"Are we getting closer, do you think? To making music with the animals."

"We have so far to go," he cautions. "Glad you are on the path."

It's true, I have been on this path for so long. Not sure if I've gotten very far. We have come a long way from "Shock the Monkey."

"Peter, you should write a book on this. So much you could say."

Another smile. "I don't think so. Think about it. With music, people dance, fall in love, sing along. With words on a page, you make enemies. People turn their back on you and get ready to argue."

"I'm a noisemaker," Peter Gabriel explains himself to the crowd of scientists and tech moguls a few hours later. Everyone here admires him. "Games Without Frontiers!" "The Rhythm of the Heat!" which goes like this: "Smash the radios… no outside voices here. Smash the clocks… do not tear the day to shreds. Smash the cameras… do not steal away the spirits…."

Music, said Zen patriarch Hua Neng according to John Cage, is a form of rapid transportation, but it is also a form of knowledge. When we got it, we don't always know what it is that we know.

I have long been fascinated by the sounds made by other creatures on this planet, wondering how we can engage with them without explaining them all away. I never wanted to translate the *language* of birds, whales, or bugs, but always wanted to join in with them in some uncertain way.

Peter Gabriel is right, if you hear the world as music, you can sing along with it, join in with it, celebrate and dance with it even while never knowing precisely what is going on.

The Rhythm and the Shriek

I thought of what could be mysterious right here and close by, still possible to explore. Many ponds are near, and now was the time to explore them.

The first sound you heard was diffuse, busy. Sometimes just a few things are happening, and in the sun those plants really get up a groove.

All outside the pond was a deep silence, no traffic, no cars, no planes in the sky. No singing birds in the sky. *Plop* the rubberized hydrophone goes down, disappears in the muck. I plug it into a little Bluetooth speaker. What? A shocking sound, there is a huge thrumming noise down there. Overlapping rhythms, shaking, expanding, combatting, unknown beats together. *What* could this possibly be?

The rhythms of plants just engaged in photosynthesis, exchanging oxygen with the air faster, with a beat. I always thought these beats were critters, bugs, tiny little insects, but the regular pad of beats is more likely a mixture a plant background rhythms and individual animal cries, that is what forms the wonderful music of ponds. You don't really have to believe in Dunn's idea of the emergent order of the pond to explain why they sound so cool.

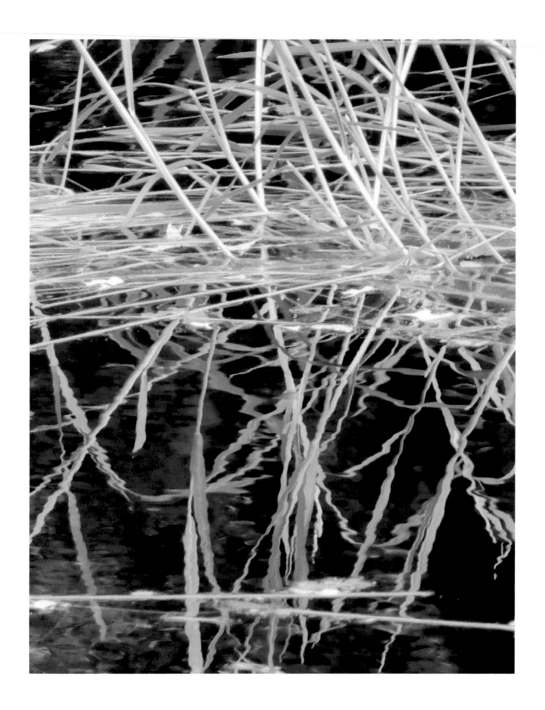

Very Rhythmic Pond
Savoy Mountain State Forest, Massachusetts

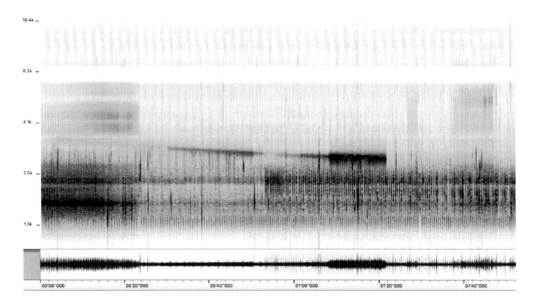

0:00 to 1:50, nearly two minutes

What a beautiful image, so clearly showing several unspecified creatures over a bed of vegetable beat. A real pond orchestra, a soundscape with several elements. You're most likely to hear something like this on a warm sunny day at the height of summer. A good test to separate plant from animal.

The beat of a sun-drenched pond filling in with lily pads. The crackling and popping follow a beat. That's strange I think, having been told how rare it is among animals to be able to follow a beat. Entrainment, this ability is called, is supposed to be limited to humans and a few species of large parrot. Monkeys, then, are said not be able to dance. Well, if that is true, how come plants are so good and creating rhythms, just when faced with the beams of the sun?

Clear thumps in the sounds now deep in the pond come from the world of plants, and the incipient growls and squeaks; those are the contributions of the animals.

I was starting to hear the difference. But exactly what was I hearing? I sent the recording to the Museum of Natural History in Paris, to Jérôme Sueur, one of the world experts in bioacoustics, the study of natural sounds. He is particularly interested in assessing the sound of whole environments, rather than individual species, as a kind of indicator of systemic health.

Do certain sounds suggest a healthier ecosystem? Are other sounds warning signs of natural decline? How can we use this sonic information to better understand the world around us, so we might save it and not imperil it? A worthy and rather new science, propelled by our increasing ability to record large amounts of sound, and our technologies' ability to sift ever larger amounts of data to identify patterns, normal ones and anomalous ones. Once we extract the information from the world, we must learn what to do with it.

I was sure would be able to help me. But apparently not.
        "I don't know," he shrugged. "No one knows much about what you have heard. In fact," he wrote dispassionately but I suspect he was smiling as he typed, "we only know 10% of the sounds you can hear in an average pond."
        Ten percent? In 2019? How could this be true, with all that science has achieved? We don't know what is going on in our backyard and woodland ponds? That means ninety percent of these wonderful sounds are a music mostly unknown.

So what if we cannot identify every creature, every scary sound in the night? In music we often do not know the source, we can't explain it away, we don't know what instrument produces a sound. We may be more likely to hear something beautiful, something musical, if we don't know where it comes from or who has made the sound.

The Loudest Penis

Back to the pond, what tools do we have for understanding? A hydrophone, the underwater listening device, is a rather simple technology, but sound is an unreliable source of information underwater. We cannot tell where a sound is coming from; there is no directionality when a sound is recorded underwater, no sense of stereo separation. Only near, and far.

Henry David Thoreau, America's most famous pond-listener, had no hydrophone to dig deep but he listened all around his waterside home, and he was particularly interested in sounds he could barely hear, things faraway and vague. Those sounds right at the edge of our comprehension might in fact become the most interesting. "All sound," he wrote in *Walden*, "heard at the greatest possible distance produces one and the same effect, a vibration of *the universal lyre*, just as the intervening atmosphere makes a distant ridge of earth interesting to our eyes by the azure tint it imparts…"

A sound is ever more evocative when we know not what it means. That is why music is more accessible than language. Like Peter G told me, you cannot argue with it because it is not making any particular point—it just is, beaming to us from the thrum of the world, the universal lyre inside of everything, this animate Earth, this booming, living pond. I just want to sing it into being by telling you that you can go out and listen then make music with it too.

Pythagoras came up with a word just for sounds whose source could not be found; he called them *acousmatic*, and I sometimes wonder why he thought such a concept deserved a name. To paraphrase Robert Irwin, hearing is forgetting the name of the thing one hears.

Sometimes when you put a name on something you no longer yearn for it, as in, "Ah yes, that's a red-bellied woodpecker." Information, wrote Jaron Lanier, is alienated experience. He meant that turning feeling into data will suck the life out of things.

Out of the rhythmic pond rumbles come a series of scraping beats, the kind of sound you can make with a stick running down a *guiro*, that round wooden instrument from Cuba or Brazil, whose name comes from an Arawak fruit. Man is it loud. So loud that I think something is wrong with my machine...

Hidden Lake Water Boatmen
Fahnestock State Park, NY

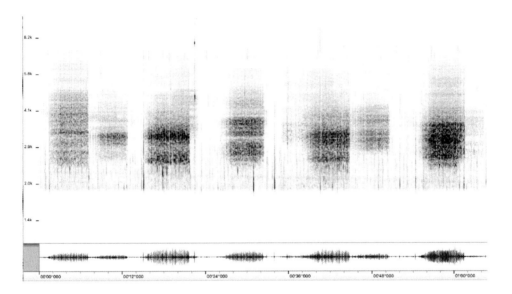

0:00 to 1:00, one minute

The battle of the penises, pond life's most amazing spectacle: three water boatmen rubbing theirs against their bodies in an early spring display of territory and attraction.

In this time of year there is the greatest rhythmic battle among the *Corixidae*. I believe I see three distinct individuals at work (or play) here. Once I see them, afterward I can hear them.

Turns out I'm not the only one who thought that. When these sounds were discovered by a man in England named James Windmill, he was sure a malfunction in the wires was the cause, for one, because they are nearly as loud as a whale! Up to 85 decibels. And it turns out these rhythmic noises are made by a tiny critter called the lesser water boatman, rubbing his penis against his own body.

Do not, I cannot stress this more strongly, try this at home.

What is a person to do with such a fact? It is certainly a part of this secret underwater pond sound story already gone viral in the online sphere, after Jérôme Sueur and Windmill published their paper "So Small, So Loud" in 2011.

Very often, the larger the animal, the larger the sound he can make. But not in the case of the lesser water boatman. He's a real outlier, and we hardly know how he is capable of such volume. Sometimes extremes make good examples… what an amazing story, and an amazing noise.

It's the most famous pond sound story yet. And it's not all that difficult to hear for yourself.

These water boatmen, of the family *Corixidae*, comprise 500 species worldwide. They tend to be found in the littoral zone of the pond, the shallower water with the densest range of plant and animal life. Some species feed on plants and algae, using strawlike mouth parts to inject enzymes into plants. The enzymes dissolve the plant material into a liquid that the bugs are then able to digest.

Most species, though, are predacious, meaning they attack and consume smaller insects. Among predatory pond insects, there are engulfers and piercers. The water boatmen are piercers.

Sometimes they themselves are eaten by newts.

Undersound

Soon after it was early 2020, I was supposed to travel the world playing live with birds. But then a global crisis hit and no one was allowed to go anywhere.

The world got quieter, no more airplanes in the sky. No more commuter traffic, no more buses and trains. The old sounds came back. The birds seemed louder; Carolina wrens next to my window in the morning waking me up in springtime. Or was that a mockingbird faking the Carolina wren? One never knows, do one. Oh, one knows all right. Depends how much you know. Depends how long you listen.

Our lives soon fell into static routines. Each day the same: Get up, take a walk outside before too many others get the same idea. But everyone already has the same idea—there is nothing else we're allowed to do.

If you do toss a hydrophone, by the way, be sure to hold one end as you swing the other like a lasso out into the wet. Otherwise, you'll soon find yourself wading out after it and scooping up muck hoping to grab the wire in your messy hands. I've done that more than once, and it's easy to feel ridiculous as the bottom feeding ducks and Canada geese, given up on migration to sit out the winter, laugh at you as you paw fruitlessly at the mud hoping to retrieve the lost and precious device that lets you hear these tiny vibrating penises with such glory. Yes, technology is a wonderful thing, isn't it, if it lets us hear incredible sounds right down the line.

Why didn't I know the water boatmen were right here, hiding in plain sight? Same reason you didn't. I had read, researched, written, but I hadn't bothered to listen.

Listening is a whole other animal… It reveals things alive before we can claim them.

I know that those who are fascinated by these sounds love what they hear. Listen for the tune of a healthy body of water, a thriving pond not a dying pond. The clicks, pops, and noises lie beneath the great silence of the brackish waters behind our homes in the woods. Suburbia contains multitudes; I am reminded of that ant war in a California suburb where massacres were occurring just a few feet away from innocent people enjoying a barbecue.

Werner Herzog looked into the eyes of a grizzly bear and saw nothing, only the cold, relentless hunt for food.

I played his daughter a recording of a magical, dancing pond and she said, "take me to this landscape."

Listen to these whole other animals and plants.

The rhythmic bubblings that easily frame a beat are like the tiny round bubbles in a fizzy drink, the even documents of carbonization. A tiny trail of pops blinks upon the water's surface, dunk the microphone and hear the *pop pop pop* of a living beat. The water lilies are breathing. Carbon dioxide. The green growing things sigh of relief and want to save the world. The tap-tap-tapping of a blind man's cane.... Indicator in the deeps. We want it to tell us something important, and will keep measuring as long as we hear a sign that the water's alive.

Still, it is damn hard to tell which plant or animal is making which sound. In the pond, we hardly ever see what we are hearing.

I want to hand out hydrophones to little kids and watch them toss them in and start to listen. Soundfishing! Let the next generation invent names for what we hear... I imagine hundreds of children, students ages six to sixteen, tossing these waterproof baubles into the muck at the end of twenty-foot lines of cable. Plug them in to whatever device you've got, and, voila, a booming, buzzing confusion of remarkable sounds. Even in this century where everything seems possible, morphable, changeable, hearable, findable at a moment's thought, there are still sounds around us in a time when we are forbidden from going anywhere, immediate sounds that we still don't know.

"Shift your attention to immediate sounds," says Crow to Hoss in Sam Shepard's *Tooth of Crime*. "Razor leathers, very razor." The characters in his play make up their own language to hope music will save the world. No matter how hard I try, I can't forget those lines forty years since Sam came to my university to try to whip us undergrads into shape. I think he lasted about one week.

Now today, students might figure all this out on their own. Let them loose on the secret sounds of ponds.

Collect all these soundfish; try to organize them. Tag them on the machine with the label *Undersound* and when the assembly approaches three hours, perhaps I have enough. Hours stream along, symphonies of the unknown. Just as the performance grounds of the Nashville symphony become overrun with hundreds of screaming purple martins, my normally silent ponds offer up their endless arias of the season, the reach of alien music into our world.

"Take me to that landscape"— but how? These sounds evoke a place, a place where few have been. When science tells you if you are right or wrong, do not deny your own experience or ideas, but try to blend information together with fiction. Make no mistake. I do not deny the fact of what can be known about the invisible underwater world. Like hearing music in the wind, I simply want to find out what it is we can all *do* with the reality of this immediate but unknown sound.

I perform for the invisible, the forgotten originators of music. Sure of their path in life, the march of evolution, these tiny creatures know exactly what kind of sound they must make. Humans are never so sure… of anything. That's why we are the ones who become philosophers.

My book *Bug Music* argued that insects were the first drummers. For millions of years before humanity, these myriad tiny creatures evolved a world of complex rhythms to further their kind. Human music emerged in forest and veldt, figuring out beats and cries in the midst of a longstanding, thrumming insect world.

All these different species doing the same things, living the same way, with just *tiny* differences. Like all those house sparrows, look at our species as if you were another species, and we'd all look the same, just like all those birds look to us. Well, I too want to be original, that's why I sometimes call myself an artist. I seek my inspiration in places no one looks, like beneath the surface of a muck-filled pond. But I know you are all listening for the same thing: something new! But not *too* new or you wouldn't even want to hear it.

I cast the microphone into the muck with a lasso-like throw, though usually inelegant, an oft-botched ring toss. *Plop!* It goes down. Old professor hydrophone. Technohaiku.

If not precise enough for science, then certainly fine for art. I take them home to the studio, play them back and tweak. Take out the noise, put in more noise. Filter unwanted frequencies, massage those that remain. Resonate, add some pitch or tone. The flickering beats of breathing plants invoke some kind of electronic gamelan. There *is* music here, a music few before have ever noticed or chosen to feel.

Little Pond Beasts with Clarinet
Pond Beasts and Plants recorded at John Allen Pond
Fahnestock State Park, NY

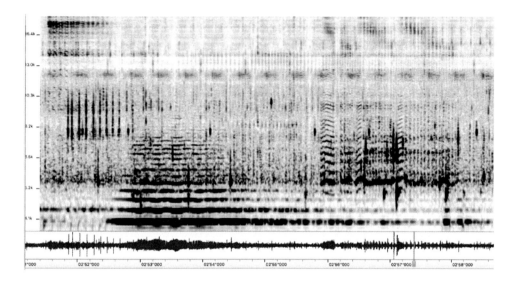

2:51 to 2:58, seven seconds

The orchestra, surely, is complete. It certainly doesn't need me, but I take it as a place from which to begin.

The human tone engages with the secret world of pond sounds. Interspecies musicians want to ensnare music out of the surrounding sounds. I want to combine my very different clarinet sound with this music of ponds. We've heard animals, then plants. Then a human instrument. It's something else.

This soundworld is busy, beating, thrumming, pulsing, all on its own without any transformations. This is the first piece where I add my own instrument to the pond sounds and feel that it works. So much goes on beneath the water. Its bustle implores me to slow down, relax, get lyrical for a change.

A minute and a half in, that pitched *guiro* again. Before writing about it, I play around it.

I'm happy being here. This is the pond of ponds.

Thrown behind bars for his resistance to the status quo, Thoreau was bailed out by his pal Emerson who cried, "Henry David, why are you in there?"
"Ralph Waldo, why," smiled our pond-dweller, "are you out there?"

I wake from a dream enveloped by imaginary rhythms and tones. *Write this down*, I gasp. Remember this midnight word: *endurance*. In the morning I do remember the word *endurance* but am not sure why I thought it was so important. Thinking back now, one day later, I feel I do know; what I meant was—persevere, last, follow your heart, delve into your obscure, sail on.
Emerson famously rode a clipper ship to England and came back to America on a steamer. He was not satisfied with the return trip. "What was missing, Ralph Waldo?"
"I long for…" he paused, "the Aeolian kinetic." The feel of wind.

When in doubt, as autumn burns, far from the booming and buzzing of spring, I click a button and let those pond sounds play. Each time they get more familiar, whether in their raw original form or transformed and transposed. I am learning, over time, to distinguish plant from animal. The plants keep time, and the beasts carry a tune.

The possibility of these sounds sometimes wakes me in the middle of the night. Maybe they can be, for me, those essential sounds that go on inside the mind *when all other sounds are cut out*, in those midnight hours of almost silence. My Tibetan monk teachers in Nepal taught me the circular-breathed tones of the Buddhist oboe, the *gyaling*, are the inner musing of a reflecting mind. For John Cage it was the hum of his nervous system and the beat of his heart, inside the anechoic chamber where no sound could survive. For me it's the surprise one hears whenever a hydrophone is tossed into a pond. Will there be something rather than nothing?

I remember visiting the great educational psychologist Howard Gardner at his office at Harvard, when I was a fairly young student. He was investigating how elementary school kids would invent their own musical notation, without knowing much about real musical notation. The kids would draw lines, up and down, and some would draw individual notes to connect with what they could play. Some were more advanced, others less.

I told him I was interested in something else, the aspects of the sounds they wrote down that musical notation does *not* contain, like the timbre, the color, some of the things Paul Klee drew on in his "Steps to Parnassus" work, where he imagined a future abstract art as stylized and strategized in the abstract as music. I have been exploring such imaginative notations ever since then, and my fascination with the sonograms you see here surely descends from those days. I want to play unknown pond noises for kids and let them imagine the monsters that make such sounds. Why not? Grownups don't know what's going on down there—*you* have a chance to figure it out.

One more small thing that the next generation has the chance to explore, along with fighting climate change and ending inequality. We sure haven't solved those problems, and I feel ever lost just thinking about them.

As autumn descends I already look forward to next spring's surge of sound in the ponds. But right now, things are getting quieter, as the birds and bugs calm down and the leaves fall red, yellow, brown, and green, the season of natural quiet soon comes. Time to hunker down and delve into the stream of sounds. How much can be found in a single minute, a single second? How does an animal take his rhythm from a plant? Everyone has to breathe and to make a world out of light. Photosynthesis, in the pond, has its own tonality. The tingle from the pond sound world makes me shiver a bit.

I have always said that my work playing music with natural sounds might increase our sensitivity and joy with the more-than-human world around us, and our sense that humans are always interacting with our surroundings, even as we try to figure out what counts as art.

At an entomology conference in Missouri once I heard a Russian expert on the sounds of one particular beetle explain, with heightened emotion, how unique the sounds of one particular critter were. In fact, she may have been the only person to ever hear such a sound. I forget the details but she was conveying the deep satisfaction she felt when first hearing this sound. It is unlikely any other human besides her will study this same sound, because there are literally millions of other insect species out there waiting to have their habits discovered.

Pond Pioneer

The pioneer researcher on these astonishing underwater sounds was a Finnish researcher named Antti Jansson. Although his name cropped up often in lists of references to the underwater stridulation of pond critters, it was difficult to learn anything more about him until an online search came up with this obituary in *Entomologica Fennica:*

> Antti Jansson's research centered on the water boatmen of the family *Corixidae*. His M. Sc. Thesis discussed the adaptations of species living in the highly fragmented environment of small rock pools. Soon he became interested in sound production of these insects, and his first paper on the subject from 1968 discussed the daily rhythm of stridulation of one of the rock pool species. His doctoral dissertation was on stridulation and its function in species of genus *Cenocorixa*, the main results were published in a series of important papers, which made him a noted specialist on insect bioacoustics. On returning to Finland, he started studies on stridulation of *Micronecta* species, and even used the recognizable species-specific differences as environmental indicators.

Ah, the recounting of a scientific life: Jansson did his homework, he found his exact topic, and delved deeply into it, deeper than anyone else had previously gone. Why Antti, why? If the sounds could tell us something about the quality of a liquid environment, the research can become that thing ordinary people might understand: *useful*. The final paragraph of the obituary is the only part that gets personal:

> Jansson had a surprisingly complex personality. Outwardly he was sociable and cooperative, as his work with a multitude of colleagues well proved. He performed his various tasks in the university bureaucracy with surprising efficiency. He carried on his research tenaciously in spite of injuries which forced him to resign his office. With his closest friends, a boyish streak became apparent, he was apt to playful jokes, even mild mischief. However, *hidden was a surprisingly sensitive personality, who could long brood on his setbacks.*

After all those years listening to the patterns of water bugs, he still knew the great conundrum of science: we will never be sure, we will never figure out the exact meaning of the biosphere. Science traffics in statistics and probability, too rigorous to ever be exactly sure, or to publish without data. It was not designed to bring us to that place of certainty where the world is precisely known.

What was it that troubled Jansson? What were the struggles that kept him brooding? When I began research on this book, no one knew what had happened to all of Jansson's recordings, the data that gave weight to his surprising discoveries. While asking around, with some sleuthing by my acoustic ecology friends in Finland, eventually we were able to find them. Now we must listen.

In 1976 Jansson wrote the first paper that described the details of the rhythmic sounds made by water boatman beetles in North American ponds. He published this in *Annales Zoologici Fennici*, a Finnish journal. Just think, thousands of miles away from where they sang, these tiny American bugs were getting their music noticed. His conclusions seem simple, even though they took years to reach. They are thus: In many species, both males and females make sounds. In most species, they tend to make a very narrow range of sounds. Males respond one way to females, and another way to other males. Some species seem, in contrast, to respond to all kinds of sounds, not only those of their own species. There is more sound in spring and summer, when the insects mature. There is more sound at night, when the plants are quiet.

This photograph was taken in Lost Pond not far from my home. Tiny, but easy! But just a few decades ago, Jansson had nowhere near the level of technology we now possess. Given this limitation it is amazing what he was able to achieve, lugging around large recorders in inclement weather with boxes and boxes of fragile tapes.

I look at the graphics contained in Jansson's paper and immediately I smile:

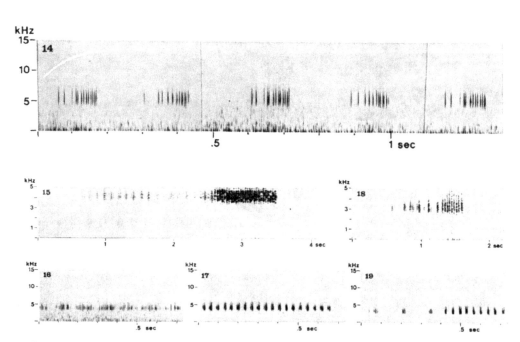

Figs. 13 – 19: *Trichocorixa naias, Callicorixa audeni,* and *C. vulnerata* signals. 13: *T. naias* male call; 14: Detailed analysis of part of *T. naias* male call; 15: *C. audeni* male call (specimen from British Columbia); 16 – 17: Detailed analysis of *C. audeni* male call in Fig. 15, parts of first and second pulse-train groups; 18: *C. vulnerata* male call (specimen from British Columbia); 19: Detailed analysis of part of *C. vulnerata* male call in Fig. 18.

I see rhythms, patterns, regularity, music, the code of rhythm, underwater, unheard, unknown by humans, until we delve down under the surface and divide to listen. He saw them also. The fuzzy black and white sonograms, printed on thermal paper, destined to fade and crumble just a few years after printing. I'm sure none of these original printouts survive today.

The paper is an enumeration, a catalog of all that he found there. He tried to find out when and why the male bugs were calling; evolution has long told us why: attracting a mate and defending one's space. The function, as with birds, as with whales, does not explain away the music. The music remains in the quality of the sounds themselves.

Jansson seems to have been a character, truly obsessive. He made a recording once every single hour to record five more minutes of water bug songs, through the entire frigid British Columbian winter night. He took his critters into the laboratory and hybridized one beetle with another, just to find out what kind of sound such a Frankenstein insect might make! I hope he would be happy that decades later some of us are poring through his tapes and his notebooks, trying to listen to the raw materials of his story in order to hold onto the receding naked songs of Earth....

I want to convey to you what it *feels* like to know these subaqueous rhythms exist, that they seem musical, these sounds that we rarely get to hear even though we know they are there. Rhythm is repetition; as things repeat a groove is born. This text repeats itself; all my books repeat themselves, saying the same thing all over again, more relaxed and with more conviction over time, by no means necessarily better or more fresh: there *is* music in us and around us. You will hear it in the most unexpected places. Each species I approach ends up transforming my own rhythms, those in music, those in words.

The scientific listener in me wants to figure all this out. The musical listener wants to feel the artistic possibilities in what is found. Here's a sonogram of a few of these *Corixidae* species that I heard at Lost Pond in Russell Wright's estate now preserved as Manitoga. Over several minutes a slow, detectable uneven rhythm clearly emerges:

Lost Pond Mystery
Strangely regular sounds from water bugs, fish, maybe turtles...

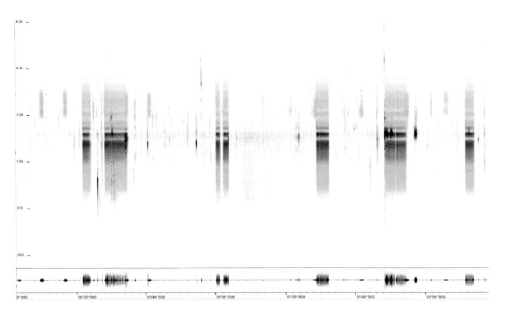

0:00 to 2:20, nearly two and a half minutes

Compared to most insect beats, this is reaaaaaaaallly slow, though nothing like the seventeen years cicadas have to count before coming in. Each rolling beat is forty seconds away from the next! Complex incredibly loud rhythmic pulses inaudible from above the surface, a rhythmic dirge deep down, almost an imperceptibly slow march. It reminds me of the superslow beat of fin whales, each of whom makes a low *whoomph* every two minutes, sped up it becomes a beat we can dance to. In this sonogram we clearly see the rhythmic arrangements of these pulse trains, they also sound like the echolocation clicks of foraging dolphins. But bugs do not use echolocation... or do they?

Zoom in on one of these loud knocks and it looks even more cryptic:

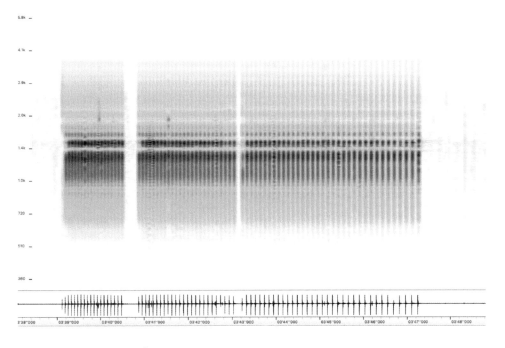

3:38 to 3:48, ten seconds

The successively slowed down *thrum*, the bug goes ever largo, starting, stretching, expanding, like a single morphing phrase of a mockingbird, exploring the possible beat he is able to achieve.

Perhaps it's not an insect, but a fish. Or a turtle. I smile to realize that even in this nearby and accessible pond, no one really knows the answer.

Sit long enough by this midsummer pond and all kinds of creatures appear. The head of a skink peers up from between rocks. I know these reptiles are common, but I never see them. In the field the sound is rough and hollow, often silent, empty, repetitive mostly over the longform time. This is a thirty-minute recording, mostly space between sounds but the pond is alive.... Mists rise inside me, that's why I add the swirls in the mix, the resounding tones, echo, resonance, you can't place it because it doesn't come from an actual object from my own mind that wants to find meaning in the emergent, in the patterns of our world that might only be there because we want them to be. Or they might indicate a yet-to-be realized order of the pond ecosystem.

This recording is quite spacious in its original form. Now I want to fill it in with drip drop drips of the undetermined. You look at it, you listen to it, you decide if there is any grand plan there, or just the beat of ambling noise—*three* not two.

The crackles in the pond go on, the shake, the separation, the silence. There *is* a rhythm down there I know it. I feels it. I wants to be *in* it.

Toss on some human effects, add the thrum. An *unidentifiable* hum, not a useful hum. (Why is it not useful to engage?) Don't ask me what pitch it is, what note, what *rezz*. Resonating the click with a hum, adding recognizable tone. A quick breath, I want to add also. Put a clarinet on it. That's how I plan to make it my own.

The Water Kobold

Now I want to play less. Ever fewer notes. Play constantly, over and over myself. Then cut it all out, leave space. Compress. Make the tones even, all the same volume. Make it sound like I wrote all this down even if I improvise. Simple pentatonic tones. Easy music. No bird would seek such simplicity.

Wheech! A shriek, a high squawk, silent again above the surface. No one has any idea at all what it could be....

A sea monster inland, a dreaded pond *Kobold*. Creature from the green lagoon. All part of the tapping, scratching, crawling sound.... Everyone is listening down there.

The Kobold is an interesting character from German mythology. Some live in houses, some in the forest, others are spirits that one hardly ever sees, living deep in the mines or even inside the rock itself. Nineteenth century miners heard their mysterious sounds in subterranean tunnels. They are often silently beneficial, but other times evasively sinister.

The element cobalt is named after them, because of its tendency to poison or pollute other minerals in a mine.

One type found by sailors is the *Klabautermann*, which sounds suspiciously like "water boatman." They are said to be especially useful at sea in times of danger. If you feel their presence, it is a good thing, but once you see one the connection is over.

Goethe recognized their importance, and wrote in *Faust*:

> Salamander shall kindle,
> Writhe nymph of the wave,
> In air sylph shall dwindle,
> And Kobold shall slave.
>
> Who doth ignore
> The primal Four,
> Nor knows aright
> Their use and might,
> O'er spirits will he
> Ne'er master be.

No bard celebrates the *pond* Kobold. Hardly anyone knows they exist! Perhaps he or she is like the German water spirit *Undine*—best left alone, but if met, you will fall in love with her, and she will have to kill you.

Here he is in Savoy Mountain Pond:

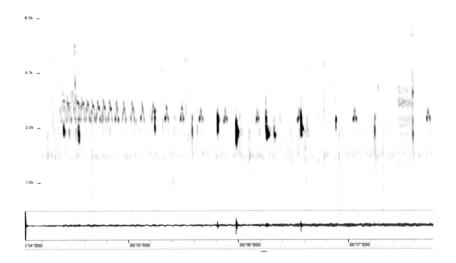

Here she is in a windswept tarn in Newfoundland:

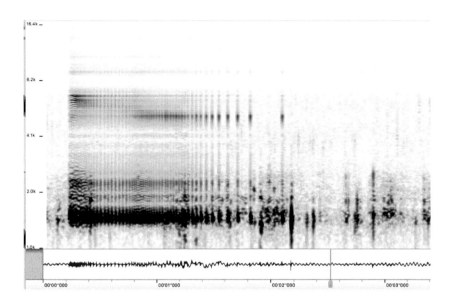

Everywhere it is a shapeshifter, a chimera, someone totally different. Always a momentary gesture, not to be heard again, in between acres of silence.

My friend and fellow pond listener Ben Gottesman tried to categorize these cryptic types of single noises in a pond in Costa Rica. Each is presumed to be a separate, distinct, and unknown creature. These are the categories he came up with:

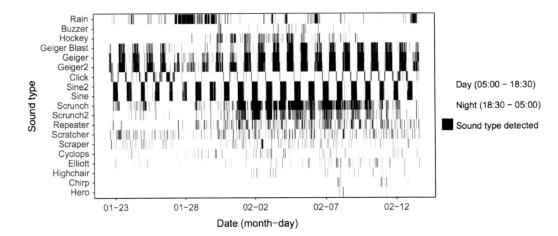

Cyclops, Highchair, Scraper, Scratcher. Scrunch, Scrunch2, Hockey, Buzzer, Geiger, Geiger Blast, Rain. *Rain*—at least we know what that one is. The others: tone after tone of undiscovered things.

This meticulous paper's main conclusion: tropical ponds are a lot noisier than we thought with all kinds of unknown sounds that we might as well classify according to what they sound like, because we do not know who or what is making them.

Here's how I started to interact with these obscure sounds and creatures: I put Ben's sounds into a software drum kit and started playing the hits back and forth in different rhythms, trying to inhabit the power of the noise. What beats did they suggest, how might I rearrange them and dance to them? Then he told me to stop. His advisor controls all those sounds and doesn't want them loose. No one should know. We can't let these unknown scrunchies out there. What would people think? What if someone understands them or knows who is singing? Let the high walls of science keep them in—for now. I was beginning to collect my own assembly of unknown sounds, which I am happy to share.

It was Ben who ignited my interest in the shimmering underwater sounds in ponds, after I had learned that science knows hardly anything about them. Sueur had turned me on to his student Camille Desjonquères, who was on a postdoc studying noisy fish in Wisconsin, and Ben was finishing up his PhD at the Center for Global Soundscapes at Purdue. A call for a museum exhibition called *Depth* had just been announced for the new Science Gallery in Detroit. I suggested we all collaborate… on something dark and noisy. Something whose form we could not yet imagine. Something called *The Secret Sounds of Ponds.*

These two are great examples of the new kind of scientist that the system is starting to produce; creative, curious individuals who are not afraid to extend science into art. Ben wanted to expand his research into art installations, and once Camille heard about the possibility, she was ready to join. Sure, this topic might be specialized. But it's also fun. Not finding all the answers doesn't mean you can't present the questions as strange noises and wonderful tales.

The Science Gallery is a new kind of museum, started at Trinity College Dublin, created and run by the unique leader Michael John Gorman. Michael John realized a few things about science museums and art galleries. Why are science museums usually seen as being for kids, while art galleries are for adults? Well, only the latter has expensive things on display that kids can't afford, but that can't be it. At the same time, we know science is real serious and supposed to take years of study to do, but it tells us how the real world really works, and art, well, as they say, "even a kid could do that." Today there are Science Galleries scattered all over the globe. Detroit is the first city in the USA to get one.

In the inaugural Detroit exhibition, the theme was "Depth," so immediately I thought an underwater pond full of kobolds could work, if I could have some help. Our team was now two scientists, one French, one American, and one pond recordist, me. We added an exhibition designer also from Purdue named Casey Synesael who figured out what it should look like. The task was to convey what it must be like to be inside a pond, deep in a murky world that contains so much strange music.

We want to create a *hyperpond*, something more lush than life, where you might crawl in and experience a cavalcade of lilting unknowns…. Neither known unknowns or unknown knowns, but rhythms and squeaks you could experience from the inside out. It's probably not enough just to listen, our ears are not complete enough for that. There should also be something to see….

Camille dared to ask… how to make sense of all this underwater enigma and tried to categorize it all. She wrote a fabulous thesis at the Museum of Natural

History in Paris trying to categorize all underwater pond sounds and is the one person who knows firsthand what a difficult task this turned out to be.

I asked for some of her sounds and she obliged. I asked Camille to speak her discovered facts as if a poem—slowly, with feeling:

> When you drop a hydrophone in the water, you step into a whole new world of sound that is completely different. It is hard to visualize all that you are hearing.
>
> This is a water beetle called the lesser water boatman, just rubbing his penis against his body.
>
> The lesser diving beetle contracts his muscles preparing to fly away. Are they warming up for take-off or is it a signal like "This place sucks. I'm outta here."
>
> In the background, the pygmy water boatmen rub their striated penises against their bodies to make this astonishing sound.
>
> In the foreground, a turtle bubbles past the hydrophone, and another kind of water boatman rubs his legs over his head…
>
> The underwater calling of the painted frog in a Paris pond in the Jardin des Plantes at night. Most frogs call from above the water, but this one calls while completely submerged.
>
> Why are water bugs more active at night? Maybe there is so much noise from plants during the day that the night is better.
>
> All these rhythms and even the faint squeals are likely to be bubbles in a pond very rich in organic matter, a lot of vegetation. The sediment is very muddy, so we hear photosynthesis, decomposition, and the respiration of the plants themselves, often more rhythmic and musical-sounding than the underwater creatures. Whenever there is a flow of energy in the plant that is continuous and regular, we hear rhythmic sounds.

Pond sound world is a mix of silence and surprise, confusion and illegibility; rhythm, squeak, and noise.

Our plan was to make a multi-channel audio work that swirls around your head as you enter the space. Originally, we thought we would use these little high-tech speakers that you can only hear when you are very close to them, the kind of thing I've seen in rad nature and science museums that built complicated environments that you slink through often in the dark. But that seemed too technically challenging, and besides, those little speakers don't produce the very deep sounds which do exist in ponds. What could we do with a simpler setup? Well, four regular speakers would be easy to control from a simple audio interface, and through those four we could run as many uneven loops of sound as we wanted. I settled on the number…. eleven.

Here's a version of what the soundscape sounded like one time, though because it was made of eleven uneven overlapping tracks, it would never sound this way ever again:

Each of the eleven tracks is a loop of uneven length, each several minutes with a bit of sound and another bit of silence. They cycle repeatedly, as long as the program is running. Because every loop is a different length the artwork will *never sound the same way twice*. Composing for such indeterminacy requires a certain kind of faith in the listener, and a certain kind of openness in the composer.

Here's what the installation in Detroit looked like:

Because I was never able to attend my own installation, I asked for a video of what it was like to be inside it:

I first learned the value of openness from John Cage. Read his great book *Silence* and you too will want to be an artist. Listening to music. Composing music. Playing music—what could these activities possibly have to do with one another? Cage the Zen master, composer as trickster. He was able to shock us until the very end of this life.

A trickster, as Lewis Hyde reminds us, is a good thing. Not Tricky Dicky from Yorbalinda (the genuine plastic man), but the trickster (coyote) who made this world. He fooled matter into being! We humans tease meaning out of the ineffable patterns of the universe that just go on and on, whether anyone listens.

Cage's Octopus

My students are mostly working-class types at my engineering university in Newark, New Jersey, majoring in mechanical, civil, computers, business, or design. They are outraged that someone could in all seriousness compose a work completely made of silence. How pretentious! they exclaim. Like that guy who taped a banana to a wall with duct tape and sold it for a million dollars! Chalk another one up to the outrageous excess of the art world.

We perform a text by Cage, "Composition as process." The master here asks a long series of questions. Here's a part of it:

> Is there such thing as silence?
> Even if I get away from people, do I still have to listen to something?
> Say I'm off in the woods, do I have to listen to a stream babbling?

So, do I *have* to listen to a stream babbling? Or a pond *noising*? I do not. I can just talk, talk, and talk.

My students critique this. They too have been inside an anechoic chamber; turns out our school has one and no one has ever told me about this! I feel left out. A few of them have been in there.

You hear thrums, you hear rhythms, pulses, a sound inside yourself. So, who is this guy to imagine there is such a thing as silence? We cannot turn off our ears. I smile: right you are. Cage too has been there. He heard the beat of his own heart and hum of his own brain thinking. The reason to stop making music is actually to better learn how to listen.

We perform these questions, record them, and remix them. Then we listen to John Cage performing them, running through Regents Park in London overlayed with footage of jazzman Rahsaan Roland Kirk, blind from birth and able to handle three straightened-out saxophones at once, jamming with animals in the London Zoo. This film by legendary music filmmaker Dick Fontaine from 1967 was probably the thing that set me on the path to animal music when I first saw it at the Banff Centre for the Arts library when I was eighteen years old. Rahsaan like Cage was so idiosyncratic as to have been basically left out of standard jazz history—no one knows quite what to make of him.

The fine film *The Case of the Three-Sided Dream* was made by Adam Kahan, and one passage shows Kirk wondering how Anton Dvorak could write such fine 'negro' spirituals being so European himself. "Some say," he muses, "Dvorak was a white man. Some say he was a black man." "Rahsaan," asks a critic, "What do you say?" "Me," he smiles an answer. "I don't give a damn."

Whenever I have found myself listening better or getting others to listen to the inimitable beauty I discover around me, those are the moments I feel I succeed.

As soon as the students listen openly to Cage performing his own texts, they realize he believes the things he is saying. And he wants us to believe them too. I have nothing to say, and I am saying it, Cage famously states. But that is not what he means. It is like Werner Herzog announcing that he feels nothing real in the face of nature, even though he can never stop questioning it. Where else are you going to find the truth of the *abyss*?

I am happy my students end up taking Cage more seriously than they wanted to at the beginning. This makes me happy because Cage meant so much to me when I was at the same stage in life that they are now. He made me want to become an artist and I hope some of them will feel the same.

It's not that I want to valorize quirky individuals over the collective march of music history. But I do agree with what Sidney Bechet once told to his Paris neighbor who wondered why he spent so many hours practicing strange animal sounds on his balcony. "Sometimes," Bechet told him, "What we call music is not the real music."

October 2020, eight months since the performing of live music has been forbidden. Friends in Iran over the years sent me photographs of billboards there announcing the illegality of music. I always laughed and then cried inside that somewhere in the world this is what authorities did decry. I never thought it could happen here, and of course when it did it was for a different reason, a sense of distress but also fear. Music was no longer safe. At least not indoors, in a quiet place, surfeiting over the silence. That was all in a world we used to know.

This was the new reality that sent me out to the ponds nearly every day, as often as I could. Nothing so glamorous as an encounter with an octopus, like that film of the moment *My Octopus Teacher*—so interesting to learn it was made from footage shot for a David Attenborough production back in 2010.

Filmmaker/diver Craig Foster thought about this year with the puss for nearly a decade before figuring out exactly how the story should be told. The close encounter of one person with one animal… same kind of thing people can feel when staring into the eye of a whale. Me, when I'm making music in nature, I usually don't feel that. There is no me and him, me and her, me and it, but my sounds together with others' sounds, live and leaping into the lap of the world.

It's not that I wouldn't want such a one-on-one contact with another creature, it's just that I don't think that's the best way to find music there. It is not an I-Thou situation, but instead the music itself is the unity, the identity, the process that is more real than the various species who produce it. It cannot be made by humans or ponds alone, but only when we decide that underwater, there is no such thing as silence, and that the soundworld we hear is on the path toward music. Our sense of what can be called music *expands*; that's always the reason I want to make art together with the plants and animals around us.

I thought this pond-derived music would sound impossibly abstruse, far beyond the likes and dislikes of most people, just a complete and utter obscurity, but actually these sounds seem to inspire as the audience starts to feel the rhythm. There are beats out there far beyond the simplicity of human time. The clicks of the plants breathing in, breathing out, make it seem like they are striving toward the need for music, without being aware of what they are doing.

The pond is the teacher, underwater lies the source. By the Awosting Dam the water is shallow, nothing looks alive. Indeed, the water is supposed to be too acidic to encourage life, but life somehow remains. I hear them even if I don't see them. I listen to the captured hours, over and over again. It becomes the natural context for my clarinet dreams. Bass clarinet. *Contra*bass clarinet. Just low, low as you can go. I try to unplay my instrument, to turn myself into a pond creature. I know nothing, absolutely nothing outside the ringing rhythm of my rippling water.

Awosting Dam Busy with Clarinets
water bugs and water lilies by Lake Awosting Dam
resonated with clarinet added

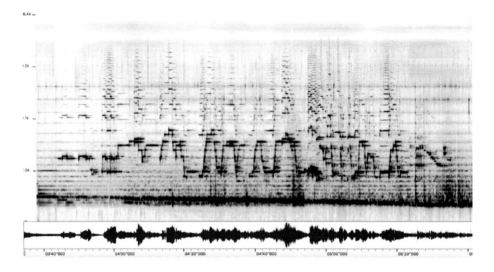

3:40 to 5:40, two whole minutes

The sonogram shows the entire final clarinet intervention, a rising and falling melody under the intensified thrum of this plant and animal pond world. The instrumental alternative to what we just heard above, when words were interred into the deep… here I was only ready to play after I had made the pond strike its own bells.

Lake Awosting, a famous destination at the end of the carriage roads in the Minnewaska Park, is a fabulous place to swim, unflinchingly wild. I had always heard the water was too acidic to harbor any fish, but it is clearly full of photosynthesis and water bugs, though different-sounding ones than I found elsewhere, more high shakers and maracas than thumps and burps.

I record the submerged sound, play it back, think about it, massage it gently into music, and wait until inspiration strikes to join along.

The piece is long. It has to be long. Because inside of the pond nothing so clear happens. It's as if the microphone is being dragged through the sand, scraping the bottom. But it is not. This is just the sum of what is down there, from the invisible silence above. I have nothing to say, and I am saying it. I am becoming the pond.

"Without dreams we would be cows in a field, and I don't want to live like that." Everyone tires of their unreachable dreams eventually. If that's the way it is, then work harder, try to find people still actually awake. I hear this all in Herzog's wry voice, the conscience of dreamers everywhere. Who can fill all of our doubts with gravitas as he speaks them, making us smile. His is not a parody of a German accent, but a voice that yearns, that still believes, but is not afraid to clearly question everything or anyone, and with all that depth still able to laugh. Why in his film *Meeting Gorbachev* the first thing he said to the man who upended Russia was "why, I'm sure the first German you ever met must have wanted to kill you!" The old dismantler of the Soviet Union really does not quite know what to say to that.

You know, even John Cage wrote of Fourier transformations, that mathematical technique that leads to sonograms, and somehow to the building blocks of electronic music. From page 47 of *Silence:*

FOURIER ANALYSIS ALLOWS A FUNCTION OF TIME (OR ANY OTHER INDEPENDENT VARIABLE) TO BE EXPRESSED IN TERMS OF PERIODIC (FREQUENCY) COMPONENTS. THE FREQUENCY COMPONENTS ARE OVER-ALL PROPERTIES OF THE ENTIRE SIGNAL. BY MEANS OF A FOURIER ANALYSIS ONE CAN EXPRESS THE VALUE OF A SIGNAL AT ANY POINT IN TERMS OF THE OVER-ALL FREQUENCY PROPERTIES OF THE SIGNAL; OR VICE VERSA, ONE CAN OBTAIN THESE OVER-ALL PROPERTIES FROM THE VALUES OF THE SIGNAL AT ITS VARIOUS POINTS.

Exactly what was he thinking about when he wrote this? I mean, Fourier analysis is how you make all these sonograms that I use to visualize unclassifiable sounds. Was Cage doing the same or did he look at images made by people who did the same?

The world is bucking up against its ability to cope, and I am in the warming spring woods listening to ponds. These sounds will send me on all kinds of journeys, virtual and real. Listen to the results and ask me how I got here. You'll want a quest too. You deserve one. Ask and you shall answer. Open the door, walk out, head for the faraway nearby, and listen....

Autonomous Sensory Meridian Swamp

When you come across a strange sound, ask not its purpose, but strive to inhabit it. This world of ponds we are investigating may be an unfamiliar world, but it is a world of sounds that can tingle us in a most pleasant way. David de la Haye, British composer and field recordist, has made the connection between these sounds and ASMR— Autonomous Sensory Meridian Response—something I had never heard of under that name though I'm sure I have long felt it. Until a few years ago my students, people who spend a lot of time online, started to really get transfixed by watching videos of women combing their hair for many minutes or even many hours.

The idea is that certain kinds of experience listening to sounds make your brain kind of feel funny, make it sizzle, make you shiver, and the pond sounds may be able to do that too. They could end up useful, could help you sleep, relax, relieve stress, and offer an overall sense of euphoria. Like the most popular music of the streaming era, they too can be useful.

The ASMR connection means that perhaps it's going to make you feel better to hear something tremble, something you haven't heard before, something alluring that you will want to hear more of once you open yourself up to the possibility of listening better, deeper, more.

With my mouth I just go *pop pop pop pop pop pop pop pop pop*. At a certain speed I go back to one of my earliest memories, a nightmare from childhood in Upper Manhattan, 315 Riverside Drive. Running to my parents' room I heard this in my head going *ah ah ah ah ah ah ah*, like the popping bubbles of plants, rhythms today in the pond. Back then it was scaring me. Now I discover sounds just like that, I don't know if they make me calm down or agitate me. Remember history, remember my past, these pops retain a certain sense of beauty, a tingle that resonated so deep inside.

I brought John Cage's ideas of listening to the world to my class. They said "all right, we'll listen to the world, only if it helps us. If it's very *restful*, if we are relaxed to have such silence all around, like a ritual experience tuning the mind."

Now we have playlists of music that help us study, that help us relax, that help us focus, that help us make love or cook. If isn't useful, today's mood goes, then we don't want it.

But wait in silence and then hear the water coming alive because of who lives there, waiting through silences of many minutes, even hours, then hear the shriek of an unknown animal—fish, insect, amphibian? You're surprised you're interested in this hunt for the unknown?

I take these rhythms from underwater in a pond and turn them into something that others will want to join in with. It's like a photograph of something beautiful that makes you notice, like this picture I took after hours sitting at Lost Pond. A frog peeps through the surface of the pond. You see the colors of the eyes, his world, the context, and you realize it's not always easy to separate the figure from the ground, as the animal appears as a wash of overlapping color, sensation, surface, and light.

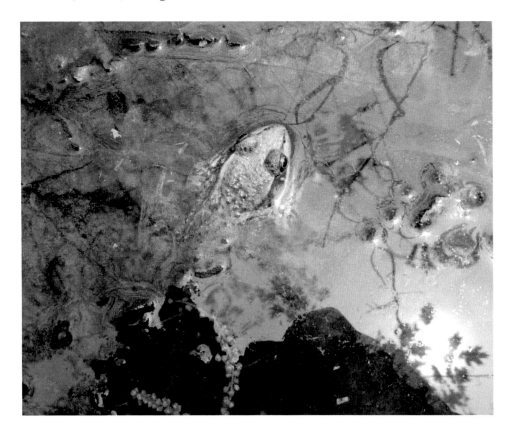

The frog, the plants, the reflection, woven in with their context—beautiful because these entities reimagine shapes, patterns, rhythms, melodies, visible and audible. Maybe they don't fulfill their full value as *things*, but as relationships or tendencies you pick out, but how it all fits together. You can't quite say where one thing ends and another begins, what rules are there, what kind of music this looks like. I don't worry about that anymore.

It's okay if it calms you down. Let the purpose of the moment find you.

The pond sounds warble and upon them I play the super-low contralto clarinet that really has that dark rounded beauty that contrasts and cushions them. Of course, I don't mind whatever purposes listeners affix to this music: let them relax, let them resonate with the deepest beyond or spirit. John Cage said "take sounds as sounds," but that was in a different time. Back then people may not have asked the sound, "what can you *do* for me?"

Regrettably all sounds are sounds, they *remain* sounds, but working with them, thinking about them, playing with them, really valuing them can mean so much more now because the techniques were accessible. We are able to play, we are able to enjoy, we are able to work with this. You just need to listen better, and the only way to listen better is to open yourself to the possibility, to go out there, ready yourself, and do it. Take the time to sit next to that pond, toss the hydrophone deep into the music.

Listen. Often what happens is nothing; there's no sound, tiny things that mean nothing, so you have to open yourself to their meaning. Little rhythms appear, minute sounds that cannot be easily transcribed or understood.

You begin to become excited by a tiny unexpected event. It could be the bubbles and movement of plant oxygen or the sound of photosynthesis or an unknown creature, something you cannot see, never see what you hear, his identity, her identity, mixing in with rhythms that make you feel enlightened, alive, electrically charged all over.

One technique I and many others use is to sample, to take fragments of it, and repeat and repeat, play, turn notes into a sound play. At the microscopic scale this technique is called granular synthesis, breaking the already diffuse sounds into their tiniest grains. If it works I like to believe I am finishing processes already started, or enhancing a tendency or aesthetic already there in Aristotle, Aquinas, Cage, Coomaraswamy. Brian Eno liked the phrase, "Art imitates nature in its manner of operation."

We desperately want to be natural; we think our tools may be natural, our food or flavors natural, our instruments might help us get there by granulating bits of insect and plant noise in a little pond at the Nature Center in Cornwall-on-Hudson, New York. That's where I got one of my favorite recordings.

Plant from Animal

Hudson Highlands Nature Center, Cornwall, NY

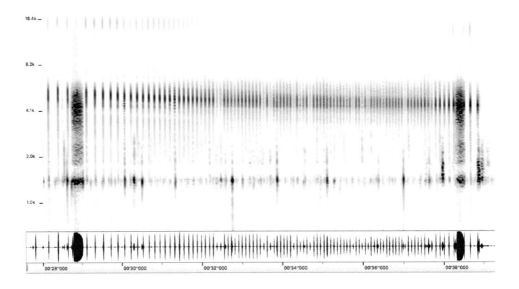

28:00 to 38:00, eight seconds

Ben Gottesman told me this is the best freshwater hydrophone recording he has ever heard. Now he's recorded ponds all over Latin America, so I am proud to have impressed him. And it was right next to a highway, Route 9W, in Cornwall, NY! Go figure.

What you see, hear are two outbursts from an animal, interspersed with an accelerated rhythm from a breathing plant.

"Looks like an animal to me," I told Ben." "Nah," he said, "that's the sound made by photosynthesis… like you slowly unscrewing a bottle of fizzy water… textbook plant."

Aquatic plants take energy from the sun just like terrestrial plants, except because they are underwater we can *hear* the oxygen being released, in the form of minuscule bubbles that often cannot be seen. The cells of leaves, either above or below the water, contain chloroplasts, which are the organelles in the cells that make photosynthesis possible. These parts of the cells contain chlorophyll molecules, that absorb light, mainly in the red and blue wavelengths. That's why plants appear green—as they reflect more green light than they absorb.

Plant sugar made through photosynthesis fuels growth, development, reproduction and repair. At the same time, photosynthesis also removes carbon dioxide from the environment and replenishes oxygen, and these are the air bubbles being released that our hydrophone lets us hear as unusual rhythms, as long as the sun's effect is felt.

Rhythm vs incident, pattern vs novelty. Two kinds of inaudible life, brought suddenly now to our ears. Repetition that gives us a beat, speeding up, slowing down, and then, the outburst, a kobold, a creature of the new world, a new musician to meet in his sonic world and ours.

So, we play it, visualize it, look at it, and just see what happens.

The late great saxophonist Wayne Shorter even spoke about this once. He said:

> The lotus flower only thrives in a swampy area, in jungles, in murky water. And when the flower blooms, the murky water around it becomes clear. So the murky water equates to the world that we live in—the spice and all that—and when enlightenment happens, the clarity starts. Then it gets covered up and starts again, and covered up. And more people wake up to their eternal potential.

I wish I had the chance to play Wayne this music. He would have smiled.

The granulation splitting sound into little pieces, spreading it, putting it on both sides of the head moves it around so it's terrific being right in the middle like a singular underwater side of the right side totally separate blur it into a cloud resonated sonic selfie blurred into a cloud. Extend the length of the phrase, more pops come in, more clicks, a little bit of sense of the original already turned to this little shivering ASMR. A little bit of a beat is there. I can take a larger loop, quantize it, but how regular do we want to be, just how regular is the world?

It's subtle, it's quiet, I'm grasping for it, yearning for it, listening deeper for it, a very low thrum arrives, put it there. I want to transpose it down down down, so you remember these water bugs whose boom can be as loud as a whale. Turn the pitch way down and now you have a beat, a pulse, a blue-whale magical 52-hertz whale, unknown species, right there evolved, evaluated, recreated from this found sound in the ordinary pond, rhythm slow against rhythm fast.

This celebration of pond sounds is not just a search for a feeling, something that encourages this ecstatic vibration all over with no drugs, no artifice, no game, changing you into something that you are not. It's a question of resonance, getting you to vibrate with the music all around you that the world seems to make.

If you aim to seek the universal in a grain of sound, then you will keep looping back to the same ideas, the same feelings, but endlessly want different sounds to to take you there. That's why we keep making music; that's why we cannot quell our urge to create.

It just springs up from somewhere.

If you become fixated on just one small thing to listen to, but want one giant step for humankind, you for example might not be surprised to discover deep in the pages of the giant five-volume epic *Truth and Justice* by the great writer of the first Estonian republic, Anton Hansen Tammsaare, glimmers of the secret sounds of a pond:

> 'Let me tell you, Mr. Luts, what I consider poetry,' said the curate. 'If here, where we stand in the darkness, we heard a patriotic song from among the bogs and marshes, sung in four-part harmony, as if from the river or the

bushes, from the fire, or from anywhere…'

'From the river bottom,' joked the clerk.

'Why not the river bottom,' the curate agreed. 'If a beautiful song about our land suddenly broke out among those bogs and marshes, that I would call a true poem.

I would take my hat off to such poetry.'

Little did they know that the very ponds *do* sing. We all missed it, for centuries.

I used to seek the spiritual, the feeling that there was something almost within reach just beyond normal experience. Perhaps the activity of pond-listening, pond-musicmaking is a spiritual practice in the end. Because every time I do it there is a connection to forces and beauty so much larger than myself. I don't play with the pond but the pond plays with me.

Reach of Resonance

This morning I picked up the old beautiful book by Rene Daumal called *Rasa*, out of print from New Directions. There's a line in there in Louise Landes Levi's fine translation: "the essence of poetry is resonance."

Resonance: you echo with something; you reverberate together metaphorically with something, and that's how it matters.

Literally *rasa* is the name for the nine forms of emotion or quality in ancient India. I remember when in Nepal as a student, 19 years old, I was obsessed with categorizing, making sense that there could be an order of things, nine rasas, nine senses that organize emotion in a poetic rather than logical way.

I'm trying to reverberate with the little world of ponds, delicate immediate ponds that are right around us. I am trying to get you to focus on these immediate sounds, easy to find. I'm going to get you out there listening, to resonate with these rhythms, find something of value there, and you're going to turn it into something for yourself.

It's called Hidden Lake, because sometimes it seems as if it's not even there:

I've been to Walden Pond many times, a pilgrimage site for environmentalists and everyone else. From my college dorm in nearby Cambridge, I often tried to borrow a friend's car and drive out there, just to swim, to walk, to revel in the incredible history. The pond is right next to a highway now, but it was already next to the train tracks in Thoreau's day. He heard the thrumming resonance of the wind in the telegraph lines and thought of the air singing along with the world.

Thoreau took the mundane experience of living by a pond and made it stand for the whole gamut of American self-sufficiency, for the conceit that we might do it all on our own. The strum of wind against the telegraph lines was echoing resonance, like an instrument that was popular in his time called the aeolian harp. It had strings that were played directly by the wind and produced an eerie overtone series like synthesizers often do today.

During these months we're not allowed to do anything else. I often hike up to the ponds to see how the ponds are doing. There is one I know that is completely dead, a gone pond, but a significant pond. I don't think it had a name. It was smack between Mount Taurus and Breakneck Ridge, the water supply of the Cornish Estate, halfway up the valley to Lake Surprise where there's a famous summer camp that both composer Morton Subotnick and literary scholar Marjorie Perloff attended, possibly at the same time in the 1930s. Sometimes unknowns become known.

This pond is no longer a pond. Its dam was destroyed by Hurricane Irene in 2011. It is the subject of a book far deeper far longer far more involved than even Thoreau's *Walden*. The philosopher Matthew Ally wrote *Ecology and Existence: Bringing Sartre to the Water's Edge*, a more than five-hundred page philosophical investigation into a pond that no longer exists, tying its nonexistence to the work of Jean-Paul Sartre, the subject of his PhD dissertation from the City University of New York.

Ally started visiting this pond nearly two decades ago, and the book came out in 2017. It has taken me these five years since then to grasp the importance of his achievement. Perhaps Ally has in fact written this book only for me, another philosopher like he who once made the pilgrimage to Norway to meet the great Norwegian environmental thinker Arne Naess, to learn what we could from him. For many years Ally was my neighbor up the road in this Hudson Valley town, and I really wish I had joined him on one of his many visits to the nameless pond above the Cornish Estate in the nameless valley between Breakneck Ridge and Bull Hill.

I was there the other day and reflected on the emptiness of the spot now that the pond is gone. In *Ecology and Existence*, a title that seems to cover all and everything, Ally admits there are two secrets about the pond. I *think* these two surprises are 1) the pond no longer exists, and 2) it was not really a pond, but a reservoir, built to provide water for those long-departed Cornishes down the road.

How he got Jean-Paul Sartre, that chain-smoking Parisian man of *ennui*, into the story takes quite a few pages to explain, but if a philosophy is to be of any use at all, we ought to be able to apply it to whatever questions that vex us.

Ally loved ponds since his childhood and remains a keen observer of what happens to one's intimate experience when you return to a place that doesn't need you, day after day:

> What, at this point in time, can we know about a pond? It seems that this question can only be answered by studying a specific case. What do we know, for example, about this particular pond? Such knowledge would amount to summing up all the data on the pond at our disposal. We have no assurance at the outset that such a summation is possible and that the truth of a pond is not multiple. The fragments of information we have are very different in kind. . .. Do we not then risk ending up with layers of heterogeneous and irreducible meanings? …

> For a pond is never an individual; it would be more fitting to think of a pond as a universal singular. Summed up and for this reason universalized by the Holocene, the pond in turn recapitulates its epoch by expressing itself in it as singularity. Universal by the singular universality of natural history, singular by the universalizing singularity of its spontaneous emergence, the pond requires simultaneous examination from both ends.

The universal in the particular—that's what we both crave. Listen deeply to a place and we can find out its lasting value, even if it dries out to the point when its pondness is no longer there.

One day Ally returns to his beloved site of probed experience and his pond is no more. The storm of the century turned inland and decimated our land. First time in anyone's memory did a hurricane turn up the Hudson and head North, wreaking havoc in its way all the way to the Adirondacks, with no mercy. So much was destroyed.

I remember that day so well. The riverbanks were high, overflowing, and people kayaked in the streets. It was the day my father passed away, eight years after he suffered a stroke during another wide calamity; eight years trapped in a wheelchair unable to move, horrified at become a patient who would never recover, forced to feel helpless in the midst of an active working, traveling, experiencing life.

On the day the pond was destroyed he also died.

Even during the funeral, the electricity had not yet come back. The rabbi reminded us that it was eight years earlier, on a day of extreme heat that the city's power grid failed, the day of the great blackout when no one could keep cool, when our systems failed my father also collapsed.

I was returning from a trip and without electricity could not be reached for several days.

The rabbi said this at my Dad's funeral, "This man suffered a stroke on the day of the great blackout, and left us eight years later on the day of a great storm. That is the kind of power he wielded." The audience chuckled. "I have no doubt the power will be restored." God endlessly renews the world.

Years before, probably when I was still in high school, my father casually told me this: "At my funeral, please play Benny Goodman's 'Sing Sing Sing.'"
I looked up, registered that thought in my mind and made sure I would not forget. Thirty years later I had to learn the part.

My father always was a Benny Goodman fan. I got a kick of the idea thinking that Goodman was somehow the Bruce Springsteen of his time, a megastar, kid from the working class who made it big. And he played the clarinet!

My dad told me earlier when I was ten, "why not the clarinet? You can play it in classical music or jazz."

He did not suggest I could play it with underwater sounds of ponds.

At my college graduation, 1984, they did not announce who the honorary degree recipients would be until they got to march along in the procession with everyone else. Giddy with excitement, my friends and I were marching to the party through the streets, playing our instruments. I had a graduation robe on and a clarinet in hand. I craned to try to recognize any of the honorees walking by. And there he was, Benny Goodman himself, getting an honorary degree!

He saw me holding a clarinet and smiled.

I remember that when Vaclav Havel, freed from prison, was speaking up for freedom and democracy for his nation the Czech Republic, he announced to the world in his inaugural speech as president, "we have to put essence before existence."

This seems to be some kind of veiled reference for the opposite of what Jean-Paul Sartre believed. He and other existentialists wanted to put existence first, so the fact we are here, we live, we are, we endure, comes before any sense of figuring out what is right and what is wrong.

Maybe that's why Sartre and his ilk were such fervent communists. In theory everyone working together, equal, did sound pretty good.

Here's how Ally orders it to celebrate his once eternal pond:

> Existence precedes essence because it's all related, all creatures and every power, the whole Earth and for all possible worlds, all intimately connected and utterly intermingled. Which means you can't think one side well without thinking the other. You've got to think in both directions at once. It's easy to

see, if only we look, easy to hear, if only we listen, easy to smell, to taste, to touch, if only we let ourselves feel it. And feel it we must.

I feel it, Matthew. Visiting the place where the pond used to be, I remember everyone and everything that used to be here and now is not. The pond ecosystem exists only through relationships, not appearance or disappearance. The pond may no longer seem to exist but the relationships that honed its evolution remain, all the way down to the tiny sounds that we sometimes can capture but have always been here, long before we deign to notice them and long after all of us are gone.

Ally knows we can never explain the richness of experience. But he needs to hope in hell that all this philosophy he has pored over for years, that he has mastered inside and offered up to his students, can help him make sense of how his surroundings can be both permanent and ephemeral at once:

> A pond is the patient work of myriads of multitudes of earthly creatures and worldly powers, a confection of life. It's just a simple pond in the woods, an elemental brew doing what ponds do.
>
> It's only a pond. And after all is said and done it spills without apology into marshy flats below where its waters perk back into brook and flow on to the river and sea. And so it goes, lake to brook, brook to pond, pond to brook to river to sea. And so it goes, sea to sky to all seas and all rivers, all lakes and brooks and ponds. It quenches the Earth, it waters the world. It's only a pond, indeed.

Buried inside this vast philosophical quest in a beautiful course of nature writing, a tender witness to an ordinary beauty so close to us.

Yes, I did play a version of Benny Goodman's "Sing, Sing, Sing" at my father's funeral. I took the old sacred recording of Benny's Carnegie Hall concert, which concluded with this fabulous tune, an unusual neo-Burundi-like beat played solo by the drummer Gene Krupa, drums alone with clarinet like some kind of primal thing, looking far back and far forward from the big swing band sound of its time.

It was just me and the laptop at the podium in the synagogue, playing looped sections of the original. I smiled, "I've got Gene Krupa in a box," with a Woody Allenish voice my father would have found amusing.

Then I picked up my clarinet and joined in, trying, for the first time, to sound like Benny, one of my distinct ancestors on the horn.

Afterwards people were puzzled, since it seemed that I had composed some new remix work for this event. "How could you do it?" they wondered. "Dunno…" I responded. I had been preparing for that moment my whole life.

Using the standard technique of electronic musicians, now easy enough to do on any mobile phone. I took a piece of the original song, probably the *key* piece, the syncopated, repeating uneven even beat of the unique Gene Krupa and assembled it into loops, effectively taking out Benny's original swingin' horn part. Then in the midst of my grief I could add my own.

This was a lot easier than speaking, talking to the assembled relatives and friends, some who had not seen me or my father for decades.

Like Peter Gabriel said at the beginning, "if you use words, someone will always be there to argue with you."

That original background track is on right now. I have never had any need to use it since, but hearing it makes me want to play along. It's a celebration of life, the perfect thing to play to say goodbye to someone I loved.

Quicksound

There is a little pond upstate by the Massachusetts and Connecticut borders. I don't think it really has a name but it's near the junction named Boston Corners. It's a spot Sean O'Grady, Lindsay Stern, Edwin Frank, and I found after we came down from a hike up Brace Mountain. We found this little body of water just off the road that just seemed kind of beguiling, so I tossed the hydrophone in, pressed record, turned it on, and began to listen.

I wanted to show them that just about any pond could offer surprising and beautiful sounds.

Boston Corners Original Pond
Near the border of Connecticut, Massachusetts, and New York

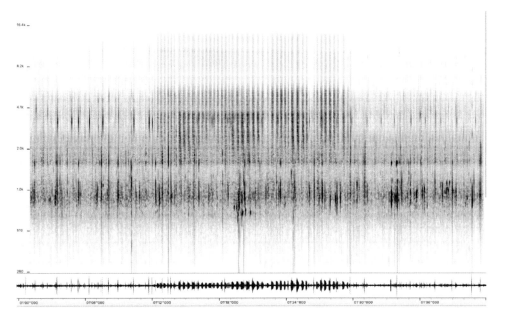

1:00 to 1:40, forty seconds

A lot of what we first hear is standard rhythmic photosynthesis, mostly plants. Then occasionally there is a little water boatman vibrational penis action and then one squirting sound that's probably a backswimmer, which looks like an upside-down boatman, or one of those pond *Kobolds* we sometimes worry about.

Backswimmer by David Michael

When the group stopped to record that little pond at Boston Corners, we didn't expect much. "Get off that man's land," Sean even worried. This was clearly a place on private property. Still, I did want to show off my quest to my friends. "Let's just drop the hydrophone in, plug in the speaker, and see if there's anything interesting."

At first it was the usual crackles of breathing plants, that primeval sound, but then there was some stridulation. Bugs rubbing parts of their bodies against other parts. And one baffling *pwoof* sound.

Just under three minutes in there came a section with shape, beauty, and form. Beginning middle and end, but still a fragment of eternity.

I wanted to transform it.

Listening to the natural rhythms innate in the recording, I ran it through an effect that literally adds tonality to the beats through a process called 'resonating.' So now in my story we have both a metaphorical reach for resonance and a technical form of resonance. It's the same word. I resonate the crackle, so it becomes just a little bit more accessible as music.

And this process helps me resonate more with the sound of the pond as found. Resonance specifically is taking a sound and tuning certain frequencies within it. Now some resonators are based on real thrums, like drumbeats, string plucks, xylophone hits or wooden marimba thunks, but others are more abstract, based on math not materials. Those are the plugins I prefer, these little add-ons to the music software, because they extract a harmony from the sound. I tweak the frequencies, it sounds alive, tonal, musical, but not so obvious, not like any actual instrument seen, touched, or heard in the actual world.

Another voice was needed.

I sent it to Laurie Anderson, one of the wisest experimenters in words and sound of our time. She said, "It is perfect," and I smiled. Then she sounded a bit like Teddy Roosevelt at the brink of the Grand Canyon: "Leave it as it is."

Next it went to Isabel Rossellini, the great actress who recently has been dressing up as various cardboard critics and enacting the most gruesome animal mating rituals. I thought she would be impressed by the notion of tiny water bugs vibrating their penises to make a sound as loud as a whale. "Please, send me more sounds!" she exclaimed. "But I don't know what to do with this."

It was time to look beyond. What performer would think such sounds are typical?

Around the beginning of the pandemic, I was supposed to travel to Norway to a gathering of the Society for Artistic Research. Like so much else, this event was not to be. One of the people I arranged to meet there was a Turkish philosopher/poet named Ilgin Deniz Akseloğlu, who contacted me through her mutual friend the artist and rock musician Alexandra Duvekot of the band Blue Crime. They were both living in Amsterdam.

Ilgin wrote to me of the concept of the "artist-philosopher" and her plans to create a School for Artist Philosophers in Norway.

She thought I might be one of them, and I basically agreed.

Since we were unable to meet, I thought I might as well send her this Boston Corners pond recording. Perhaps an art-philosophical perspective would shed light on what could be done with it.

Immediately Ilgin told me about one of her favorite writers, Clarice Lispector, the Brazilian writer, who wrote poetically on the aquatic and the liquid. She wrote a watery text called *Agua Viva,* hard to classify like so much of what I like to read, a book that tries to articulate the stream of life, what it is that makes water alive:

> The liturgy of dissonant swarms of insects that rise from cloudy and pestilent bogs…. I hear cymbals and trumpets and drums that fill the air with noises and tumult, muffling then the silence of the sun disc and its prodigy. I want a cloak woven with threads of solar gold. The sun is the magician tension of silence. In my trek to the mysteries I hear the carnivorous plant that laments times immemorial: and I have obscene nightmares buffeted by sickly winds. I am enchanted, seduced, tossed by furtive voices.

Lispector could be writing about the photosynthetic rhythms of sundrenched swamp plants. This wild music, she's going for it, aching toward a new language.

I want to turn the pond language into music and lure you into it.

Armed with insight from Lispector, Ilgin had her own take on the Boston Corners Pond. She didn't care if anyone said it was 'perfect as it is.' Depends on how much you trust the world as it appears.

Ilgin was not afraid of this sound. She had no skin in the game and was ready to try anything. This is what she did with it:

When, the Sound
Ilgin Deniz Akseloğlu, words and voice
Private pond recorded at Boston Corners

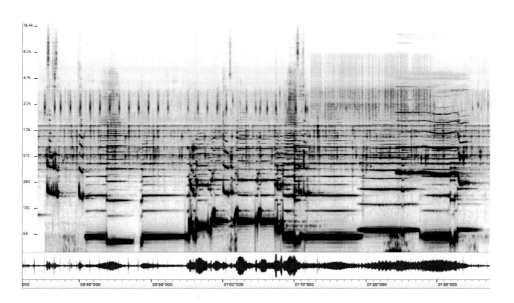

00:30 to 1:35, just over one minute

Bass tones, human interjections, and the perfect three minutes of unassailable pond. The beat of the plants and a few animals, just at the right points. Above I see harmony, perfection, proof of concept again, and my idea.

It's the rightness of pond music, most likely never to be so rightly heard again. The birth of collaboration, the sequester of love. The few-minute resonance that seemed perfect on its own… until Ilgin discovered it.

The last note is lower than the low. Here are the words the pond sound drew out of her:

> To go
> To go over this quicksand of quicksound
>
> The sound teaches me
> Now….
>
> I love you too
>
> Let's make drama
>
> *>>>>>>>aaaaaaaaahhhhhhhhhh—çıngıl çıngıl*
> *>>>>>>>aaaaaaaaahhhhhhhhhh*
>
> There is no gap—
>
> Pulls me over
> Pushes me away
> Pull me over
> Push me away
>
> When?
> Tell me when?
> I say, when
> The sound says
> > > now.

I hadn't then met Ilgin in person, but we began to talk online all the time. She was ready at once to be transformed by these sounds, as they immediately suggested to her new ideas and dissonant words.

As long as I was trapped at home, I needed to bounce ideas, and possibilities, off those I don't know and who are more excited about the world than I.

The poetic is what resonates with life but does not follow the explanatory thread. We try to play in unison but don't really want to. There has to be unevenness. The beat must never be so regular that it bores us. The swirl of sound must make us tremble.

These edgy sounds run in the background. They are the soundtrack for our journey together into an art-philosophy that only exists here and now. We have been sentenced to placelessness.

Because we cannot meet—*Let's make drama.*

We're lucky to have this wonderful voice that has not yet decided how it wants to sing. This was her first recording. Over time the texts grew more into songs.

Mohsen Makhmalbaf's film *The Silence* reveals the way the world sounds to an eight-year-old blind boy in Tajikistan. Khorshid earns his living tuning stringed instruments like the rebab and tar, but he is easily distracted, as he wanders the street and is easily lured away by beautiful voices and strangely tingling sounds. His mother advises him to put cotton in his ears or plug them up with his fingers as he rides the bus, lest he follow the beautiful voices of girls or strumming strings.

When his ears are stopped up, he hears the burbling sound of water inside his head, and as we the audience watch the film, we are easily seduced by the power of sound and the beautiful smiles and colors of the Tajik people, awash with simplicity while reeling from the ravages of the Afghan War. The film was made in 1998, but looks and sounds as if it could have come from anytime, as it reminds us who see how even the most mundane of sounds can, if we attend to them, make us shiver.

I wish I could play these pond sounds for Clarice Lispector to hear what she might make of them.

The tingling all over. The rhythm of the pond. This is what I want you to feel and be shivered by. You'll never know what makes these sounds until you realize what they can do to you.

The great electronic music pioneer Daphne Oram has this to say about resonance in her book *An Individual Note* (1972):

> Great art presents us with such a rich and perfectly controlled wavepattern that its intermodulation with our own pattern provides us with new aspects of reality…. These induced resonances in all wavebands remain with us, if renewed by memory and repeated experience…. Have you ever tried musing in front of a flickering fire? The coals form fascinating, grotesque shapes, some fiery red, some sullen black. Tongues of flame, blue and yellow, create crazy rhythms as they dance. You cannot predict what will happen next, yet you feel beneath it all a consuming pulse…. The crazy beat of the flames incites you to join them in a song: so each pathway becomes a musical phrase, each boulder a musical chord. The crescendo reaches a climax as the craggy pinnacle plunges crumbling to its death. The flickering flame is extinguished and all is as silent as dust.

Oram too was trying to explain how sometimes the artificial can sound so natural, in an uncanny way, becoming more real than sounds out there made by physical means.

Resonance as an offering can come to you in many ways. The sound, massaged or direct, can transform you even if you are afraid of the unknown. I'm always listening for what I haven't quite heard before. It might then seem I am usually bored with life but aren't we all? Enough already, we have played enough, composed enough, written enough to fill the world with excess noise. Why go on? We're still searching for something we haven't yet found.

How far can resonance reach? How much can one series of strange sounds resonate with everyone else's worries and pains? I doubt it can go so far; indeed, I wish I could explain to you the meaning and value of the greatest things.

I always admired David Sudnow's two books on how to learn to improvise on the piano. The famous one is called *Ways of the Hand* in which he tries to articulate how you are supposed to move your hands on the keyboard and know exactly what you are doing without being able to explain it, pushing for the known unknown that all those who believe in improvisation yearn for.

Few people remember his other book, that he wrote simultaneously, called *Talk's Body*, where he tries to improvise on the piano keyboard then immediately shifts to the typewriter keyboard to improvise with words. He writes about life, about playing music, about listening to the world:

> You listen to the voice to hear its nervousness.
> You listen to identify the language.
> You listen to see if you are interested.
> You listen to be able to repeat it later…
> You listen to show you are listening.
> You listen for your turn to talk…
> no thought only thinking no melody only melodying
> no itness, no thingness, only processes of sounds
> it's all a matter of form, becoming public for others
> *talk talks itself into too many objects…*
> a swarm of harmonies
> dense sounds, rich with implication….
> *sounds quiver in certain surroundings.*

Nomads with Invisible Stories

Jaron Lanier has collected every possible wind instrument in every possible size. The world's largest flute down to the world's smallest. Saxophones that can never leave the house. Lanier believes musical instruments are the most advanced tools any society has produced, because they allow us to express ideas that we do not conceive, but can only realize together with the technology, extending our bodies and thoughts into the world.

They make meaning out of the patterns of sound. These rhythms and melodies turn experience into something to love. We evolve that into language and talk about everything, but in the end it is the music we remember most.

I do just a few things to my sound files. I change the speed, the pitch, change the level of resonance, and the dial between dry sound and effected sound. Resonance vs dry/wet mix, these are not the same variables. With these simple tools I inhabit the sonic world of the pond.

Resonance is both a philosophical concept and a specific musical tool. That's one way precise actions can point toward the universal thrum. This is something humans can do: find order in the results of evolution colliding with the firmament of the physical and chemical world. The pond has all of that.

I ask Ilgin what the sounds of the pond mean to her. She is young but has seen so much, from Cappadocia to Kathmandu, from Paris to Oslo. Her art transcends genre. I ask her how she got to the words she used:

> It is dim and cold
> It feels secure since the sounds do not cease
>
> They fall like a curtain of binary code, delivering this empty room where you can dwell by yourself
> As if there is anything interesting to tell
> That's probably why I kept on saying *the sound does not listen to me*
> It's quite absurd, among all the possible existing life forms, wearing the human; wearing a zero

This has been pissing me off since I was little,
And the pond recalls it for a tiny bit, that seems funny
That's when I say, 'I love you,' *to the pond*, 'let's make drama'

I'm now a bit more relieved, following absurdity, there comes freedom
I think of the f(x) that I am and how empty I could be without the sound
All I can do is to let the outside and the inside merge without disrupting.

The chasm between us 'keeps me on hold, makes me realize there is no gap to
think by pulling me over and pushing me away'

Suspension.
Release.

I start backtracking the steps that brought me to the Sound
(with a capital S)

My feet disappear as the ground is removed
Reading words was hammering my mind
Writing words was slamming me on cliffs
Saying words was spitting soot

I left there
And I reached the Sound
It's getting softer.

Now I'm wondering how to voice the ethereal power in the soft—
The magnetic pull in the lullaby

Whatever I will do, I want to keep the rawness, the wilderness, and the imme-
diacy

On a different chord a question bounces, *What would the pond think?*

We have to hear meaning in it if we want the beauty of the pond to matter as
much as it needs to in order to save us.

Next, I gave Ilgin the "Cape Cod Long Pond" recording that began this book. Resonated, pitched down, slowed a bit so the subtleties of overlapping plant and animal rhythms come through. She improvises a whole new language upon it:

Nee-eeeeeh neeee neeee ayh ooooh

Nee-eeeeeh neeee ayh ooooh

Zooh reeeh yaaah
Zoooh darankeh naah yah —dah yah

Zooh nah kereyah
Gori vakinee

Zooreeh kimano eh

Remiso reeyeh

Sooooooooooooooooooh

Goooooooooooooomgh
Goooooooooooooomgh
Goooooooooooooomgh

Seernah
Seernah klah shhhh
Seernah klah shaah
Seernah klah shaah aay

Nerindi
Nerindi

Koomaney nerindi

Koohmaney
Koambaney
Nerindi

Koooooommmgh
Koooooommmgh

Pa pa pa pa pa pa pa pa pa pa pa pa pa pa pah

Paaaaaaaaaaaaaaah
Paaaaaaaaaaaaaaah
Paaaaaaaaaaaaaaah

Peeeeeeeey

piiiiiiiiiiiiiiiiih
piiiiiiiiiiiiiiiiih
piiiiiiiiiiiiiiiiih
piiiiiiiiiiiiiiiiih

PhShchiiiihhh
PhShchiiiihhh

Nerindi
Nerindi

PhShchiiiihhh
PhShchiiiihhh
PhShchiiiihhh
PhShchiiiihhh

Khaabaah
Kaabem
Khaabaah
Kaabem

Nerindi
Ilgin Deniz Akseloğlu, words and voice
Resonated Cape Cod pond, with Reaktor Lazerbass

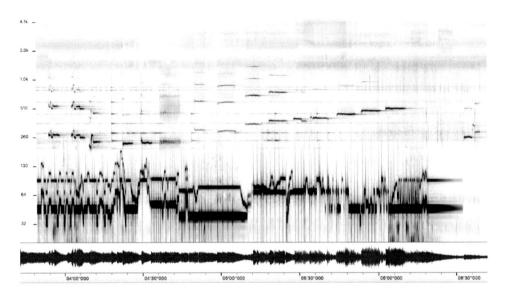

3:45-6:30, nearly two minutes

In a recent interview Brian Eno says lyrics have always troubled him. He just does not want to pay attention to the words, so rarely do they matter as much to the music as the melody, rhythm, and sound.

I wonder if he would enjoy Ilgin Deniz's half-made up, half-sensible sounds sung upon this resonated Cape Cod pond? Some are words in Turkish, some English, mostly they are the searching sounds of a singer just finding her voice, a poet-philosopher let loose in a more-than-human world of vegetable and animal sounds. Who is the mineral here? Maybe it is the sliding bass, so low that you won't even hear it unless you have big headphones or a killer sound system.

We are here exploring the acoustic niche hypothesis, where every sound has its proper frequency and space. Your sound belongs there, and mine belongs here. Is this how nature is built? It's an idea suggested by master field recordist Bernie Krause, and since he proposed it other researchers have tried to test it. Their results suggest that *sometimes* it is true that each animal has evolved a sound that stays out of the way of other sounds so that their messages can be heard.

But sometimes it's really a booming, buzzing confusion, every noise at once all around.

The aliens are here among us, right in the pond.

Nerindi... Ilgin sings. What is this word? An ancient goddess? No, a name she made up. Repeat it over and over until its meaning devolves into nothing but its own sound. It overlaps with a deep humming pond. I massage it, transform it, add just a little bit to it from the sounds I think I know.

The piece is done when I can't get it out of my head. *Nerindi. Neriiiiiiindi. Nerinnnndi?* It also vibrates, wriggling its way into an earworm. Enjoy it while it lasts. Should it mean anything in particular? She says:

> I always have the feeling I'm searching for my mother tongue.
> Who cares what words say? How they reach is what matters.
>
> It starts with some voice, near, present
> As if the voice is talking directly to the listener, there is no barrier between them. It's mysterious and yet sounds familiar
>
> Soon after, the bass starts swirling around the voice
> Unexpected, uncanny
> Like a sudden mist elevating from the ground
> Like an anaconda passing by the living room
> It helps to locate the voice.

Does the snake even want to come in?

> All the other elements keep on building up with the spell
> Nothing is left behind for the sake of climbing, nothing is rushed,
> then the voice melts into the environment and becomes a ghost—
> Only water and other beings remain.

In the next piece she writes a shadow-poem in response, a more enigmatic explanation for what this word and others mean. Here the pond sounds are further processed into a granulated stream (a technical electronic music term). So, the liner notes now appear as a subsequent piece and enter the song.

Undaunted New Lands
Ilgin Deniz Akseloğlu, words and voice
Granulated pond rhythms

1:55-2:30, thirty-five seconds

Fragments of ponds are sampled and resampled, remaking the world.

Arriving at new lands
Bringing the old to the new lands
For there is a fight against oblivion

Blessing the land
Standing firm through calling
A narrow path to settle what's vast

Nomads with invisible stories
No properties

The word is the surface of the land
Words give no hint of the tone
The melody is only an approach, a diplomacy
To give the land voice, for it can evade

Fish, birds, a river in the throes of death
By the shores of unrest
Undaunted

The colic of the bass bends the nerves
[*I'm talking about a low sound not a fish*]
And the strange chuckles behind—
Bells of a lost herd

You see, it's actually happening. The secret sounds of ponds are producing new languages, new places, new forms. But that won't stop it from continuing. There is that incessant nerve-bending bass… find a sound system that can present it.

The writer works alone. She is set at her desk, forming ideas, inventing words to mix with unknown sounds. She adds them to my in-between sounds, electronic basses morphing from one setting to the next, detuned, and exact, blending at the bottom level of our ability to hear. I want you to be enveloped by sounds you didn't realize were there, with melodies you would never notice before.

Here is where it all began:

> Hey.
> Hi.
> Hû.

> I don't know what time we are, it's a good place to be.

> I used to be a full-time surface-reader;
> The more I read, the faster the Crust spun

> Finally, the centrifuge hurled me over here.

> *Downthere*, where I left my Mirror
> The Crust is topsy-turvy, shapeshifting, shift-shaking.

> The old stratum is an untimely juvenile that meets the surface
> Stone is naked.
> Water warns with silent sirens, keeping her surge and rage inside.

> After reading too many surfaces, one day I had a dream
> The Crust was getting cracked, like an eggshell, from which Lightning has
> sprung suddenly and met their lover Water.

> The Crust is too thin now and still spinning.

> When I'm *Downthere*
> I still like watching how motion becomes a surface over the Crust;
> A gelatin interface to bounce my eyes on.

> It's good that we still look around
> Even though our noses and mouths are shut,

My skin hears this softness of motion.

Some things remain penetrable,
Like trunks of young trees,
Old stone houses,
Some people's hands have still room for joyful meetings in environments
where wood can retire pleasantly.

I don't know what time we are, but it's really a good place to be.

You made me realize better I have been here
because I couldn't give up the surface-reading until now,
Not being able to realize how distant I got.

And I still can't entirely get how distance works.

I can't measure the distance either... all these words and sounds seem so close
to us and each other, even as the process that produced them is scattered around
the globe.

It's one year later and Ilgin is trekking across the Turkish mountains and remains out of reach. I'm home back in a normalized world, sifting through all the
sounds.

Finally, everyone gets to listen to them. As in all songs, you get to decide what
the lyrics mean.

How Distance Works
Ilgin Deniz, words and voice recorded on Amsterdam's curfew streets at night.
Me, electronic completely artificial pond emulations.
Made between Amsterdam and Cold Spring.

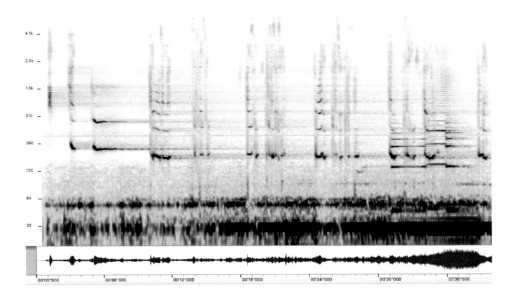

0:00-00:37, thirty-seven seconds

First I thought the pond sounds were a new source of ASMR—now it's Ilgin's voice as well, enhanced with the long echo from the Teufelsberg CIA Tower in Berlin built on the ruins of Hitler's Grünewald bunker. (No one's allowed in there anymore but luckily, we do have the impulse responses, recorded so you can add them as reverberation to any piece of sound.)

I searched for a nonpond emulation of what the pond can do—those are the nonvocal but somehow living sounds in the background, and then the contralto clarinet for reality, for gravitas.

Vacuum and Zeppelin

Sometimes I wake up in the middle of the night and know exactly what I want to write the next day or what sounds I need to play. But usually when I sit down either I've forgotten the thread, or I remember it and it no longer seems so worthwhile.

Today I'm trying to trust these gaps in my dreams that are so much more real than the inanities of the night.

The State Forest Mix is done. Built on one of my first pond recordings, made back when I had no idea what I was hearing. I didn't realize at the time that the regular blooping beats came from plants breathing and are not animals. Vegetable, not animal. Mineral is in the details, the water, the sound. I wanted to learn these beats so I sonified them further, making the beat play drum and cymbal sounds, and having the lower notes turned into bass notes. So, the data of the original swirling beat ends up playing more traditional instruments, so we the listener can see if this convinces us. Convinces us further that there is order here, some kind of light at the end of the tunnel, some kind of groove to know.

I sent it out to my distant collaborator, the young philosopher, citizen of the world, constantly thinking, wondering, knowing.

What is it that she suddenly wants to sing?

> It's the in-between dry vacuum
> (or desert) without the body
> A fortress of contemplation
> An impossible echo chamber

A lost zeppelin
A breath in an astronaut helmet

Below is too texturous
Above is full of light

Both are violent when they separate

Et voilà!

Who doesn't want to sing? I don't really myself, but I would help everyone I know do it if I could. People need to discover music in this time of rational worry and darkness. Still, no one is allowed to go anywhere; still, we foolishly believe technology will save us. Maybe it will, but it hasn't yet. Still, we are mostly all right. Still, we fear what may happen, not what has. I'm doing nothing to help. Just listening to the rhythms beneath the surface. I make them more musical by adding resonance. I remain obsessed with these first super-rhythmic plant beats from a Massachusetts pond. Trying all the different resonance formulas I know and sending the sounds out.

State Forest Ring
Ilgin Deniz Akseloğlu, voice
Savoy State Forest
rhythmic pond resonated and audio-to-MIDIed to create bass and drum parts

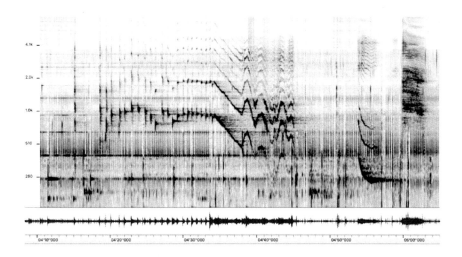

4:10-5:00, fifty seconds

We speak of the rhythm of the pond. This is what happens when that rhythmic information is changed to bass and drums. The singer of tales is let loose on it. "Play," says the enchanter. She has said goodbye to language. And hello to sound.

This recording has really made Ilgin go mad. Mad with sound, with experiment, a philosopher and master of words moving away from words into sound. I am so happy listening to this happen. She is singing above the thrum, or is it a hum? Or is it a ring, something metallic, like a digital bell. I know it's not quite a real bell because it is a digitized calculation of rings, too meticulous to be a figment of the actual world. It's easy enough to simulate the actual world. The computer contains reams of actual sampled resonance curves, maps of over-tones that explain what happens when you really strike a piece of resonating metal. The uneven evenness makes it all musical.

Those versions, though, just don't sound as good. It's as if it is better to know the resonance is artificial than to fake it into a real-sounding thing. I don't know why that is so. I keep tweaking and re-tweaking because I feel the ringing pond beat is too obvious, too clearly a voice from a machine. But maybe that's the most honest way to resonate something.

The actual is often our goal. Only once something is taken up as disembodied sound do all these tricks make sense. After that you no longer need to use the tricks. Just listen to the original and all the possibilities will sound already there.

My goal is to make the obscure important, to shift our attention to immediate sounds. Never lose the beauty of the first way these sounds strike you. Join along with them only if you want to change your life.

I zoom in on the tiny bugs, listening to them, sometimes photographing them. The camera, as they like to do today, snaps seven shots and melds them into one, trying in one picture to capture the multiplicity of movement. The beast is no stable thing.

Wildness and Wet

From Barbara Hurd's *Stirring the Mud:*

> …. You recall a line of poetry and you know why poets love the white space
> at the end of a line, how that space invites you to forgo the usual eye-drop-
> ping to the left and down to the next line. How it invites you, instead, to
> launch yourself into that white margin of imagination, where the countryside
> lies uncharted, wild habitat at the edge of civilized thinking, where the mind is
> rampant with phrases (*the opposite of stones, the sound of emerald green*) and
> you feel a certain exhilaration in the tangle and thicket of plant and word, im-
> age and water, the mind curling and leaping at the far edge of itself, tiny ten-
> drils of imagination twining their way down stems of waterweeds….

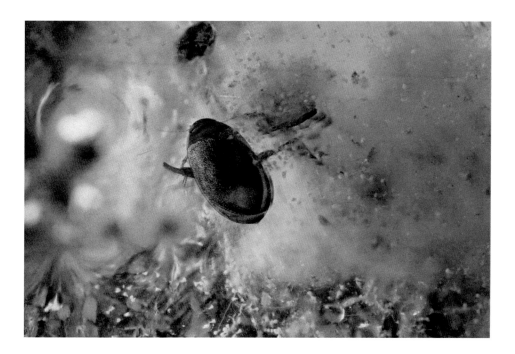

This is the edge of a mind foraging through the edge of a landscape…. No
wonder the Puritans hated swamps. Think of it this way: in sex, the more a
man disappears inside a woman, the more she feels his presence. But if you're
prudish about such things and used to banishing what you don't like, you

can't stand a damp and slippery world where the banished keeps growing,
where what's buried is so deeply felt.

Who *doesn't* love a pond, been obsessed with freshwater life since childhood,
love the feel of mud on the feet. Barbara Hurd, I never thought there was anything sexy about it, but now that I read your fine words, you know, I get it
too...

> What would the world be, once bereft
> Of wet and of wildness? Let them be left,
> O let them be left, wildness and wet;
> Long live the weeds and the wilderness yet.

Gerard Manley Hopkins got it down. When I learned those lines in college
from Seamus Heaney, I found them old-fashioned and twee. But now they
make me smile. And stand up for the experience, like an anthem from the past.

The rhythm strikes like the photosynthetic taps of the reeds and rushes. Plants
got the beat, animals the scream. That's the simple rule for the sounds down beneath.

Science knows nothing without acknowledging that we all have a love for our
subject and its magnetic beauty.

There are different kinds of precision, each glossing over the world in grand
overlays, time upon time.

The raw recordings from last spring contain the peacocking battles of the boatmen shaking their thingys wide and loud submerged, and in the distant background, looming airplanes overhead. The planes can also be heard
underwater—I remember then the shock of them, a few flights beginning after
the time of total grounding, when it seemed the world might end—those low
continuous drones are nearly always human sounds. Like right now the snow-
plow scrapes on the street, a *whoom* in the dark afternoon light. Nature and culture, culture and nature, we always think we can tell them apart, yet one is just
part of the other.

I want to listen to and learn from the world. But how can we take it all in and still believe? I've been reading three new books on what to do now with our warming world. Elizabeth Kolbert's *Under a White Sky*, Michael Mann's *The New Climate War*, and Kathleen Dean Moore's *Earth's Wild Music*. They are all fine works that speak to the planetary crisis of our time, but all of them fill me with despair, because they are all trying their best to be honest.

Look, says Kolbert, we all know CO_2 emissions must stop by 2050, and we are coming to realize that there is no way we can possibly get there without revolutionary new technologies that haven't been invented yet, and radical means of sucking carbon straight out of the atmosphere that so far seem to come straight out of science fiction. The time for easy platitudes about loving and listening to nature is long gone. We need total transformation, and that only happens fast through systemic social and technical change.

So, it really doesn't matter what kind of car you drive, or whether or not you successfully separate your recycling. She reminds us that it was in the 1960s that the Americans and the Soviets both talked about transforming the climate, with cloud seeding and reversing the course of great rivers. In the seventies this all fell out of fashion in the age of ecology, and because of Rachel Carson we ended up looking for biological controls not chemical ones to ward off pests and invasives; that's how Australia got cane toads and America got giant carp. Now we're stuck with them as we ought to remember that "you cannot fool Mother Nature."

Michael Mann, creator of the famous hockey stick diagram that whacks our emissions rapidly sky-high, tries to add a sobering note. Doom sells, he reminds us. The horror, the horror! The worse it looks, the more you'll want to read. That's right friends, feel terrible. Know it's all your fault. Give up everything you love, race toward austerity since our whole way of living must change. This idea lives deep within all of us who watched TV as kids in the 1970s. We remember the crying Indian, played by Iron Eyes Cody, an Italian-American actor. Writes Mann:

Well, when I was growing up in the early 1970s, there was a very effective advertisement that showed a Native American with a tear rolling down his cheek. He was crying because of bottles and cans littering the road. And a voice-over said, "People cause pollution. Only people can stop it."

The ad had a fundamental impact on me and a whole generation. We felt empowered to go clean up those bottles and cans. But it turned out we'd all been had. It was actually a PR stunt hatched on Madison Avenue by Coca Cola and the beverage industry in an effort to convince us that bottle legislation wasn't necessary—we just needed to be better individuals and clean up after ourselves.

In some way we like being told that we have sinned, that it is all our fault, that we are the guilty ones. Not so, says Mann, it is the system that is at fault. The big corporations happy who don't want to do anything to harm their enormous profits. They have the money and skill to easily shift the blame to individual behavior and the poverty of our own powerlessness. 95% of pollution is emitted by six industries.

In February 2023 the current owners of this ad announced they will never air it again. The time of its effectiveness has passed, though a whole generation of us will never forget it.

Kathleen Dean Moore picks a title I could use myself, as a fellow lover of *Earth's Wild Music*. Her subtitle is: "Celebrating and Defending the Songs of the Natural World." She's on the same path as I, but with more grace and fluid prose. She even takes the musical metaphor further in terms of the different ways humans can and must celebrate the world.

Moore has always been close to the land and to human emotions that flow from time spent close with it. Yet every chapter in this book ends with a gray box with one depressing fact after another: insect populations decreasing, habitat disappearing, hopelessness all around. How can we simply keep loving earth's wild music with all hope draining away?

Of course, we do have the power to organize, to get together, to share our anguish at the fate of the Earth, and to mobilize to change the systems that make things worse. That is what Kathleen Dean Moore urges:

> If you are upset about the state of things, find someone else to share your concern. Talk to them. Do not sit alone with your discontent.

That's fine advice. As writers we are used to working through our angst on the page. As a voracious reader I find myself taking in far too much, far too fast. First of all, I can recommend what moves me to others, thereby spreading the possibility for intimate experience of the word. But I'm doing research here with all these words of others. I'm trying to figure out how to explain the inexplicable. To transmit my feelings of care, wonder, and delight in the obscure magic of sounds, and innocently believe it all to matter, to matter in the midst of this time of great crisis.

You must not be afraid to listen. That line resounds in my head. It's from some play or performance out of my past, probably *The Tibetan Book of the Dead* play by Jean-Claude van Ittalie. Maybe it's a plea for every performance that exits the comfort zone; you must never fear the music—or the absence of music, or the chance for music. If told to listen for music, our ears may find music.

Last night and today brought an immense forceful wind to this village by the river, perhaps never had I heard anything like it. Not just gusts of wind but a continuous whoosh, barreling down from the North, fleecing off from the hills and into the river, pacing small continuous waves crashing against the ruins of the quarry dock, crumbling cement pieces all covered in rime, that special slick grace of the changing season… Noting all this down will not save the world, but it will make its wonder easier to love.

The pond creatures are most wondrous, to listen to, and to see. I discover a marvelous work by a Czech photographer, Jan Hamrsky, incredible photos of some of my favorite pond critters: water boatmen, water scorpions, larvae of all shapes and sizes. He published his own book, exactly his way, but is kind enough to offer up his photos to anyone, scientist or writer, who wishes to use them to help tell their own stories. These images are far better than mine, and I'm only going to show you one. The water boatman looks like a piece of fine jewelry.

water boatman by Jan Hamrsky

I *do* want to be optimistic in the midst of this warming world. Sure, I'll change a bit how I live, and imagine I'm doing my part to change the whole system. I hope to keep us all a bit more alive, by listening to some beautiful noises that are out there.

But the pond sounds speak of nothing but life, and death.

I have no illusions that listening more closely to all these wonderful sounds will stop us from destroying all the beauty that made us possible. But it can't hurt. *Maybe* it will open us up just a bit to the reality… that we should not destroy what we don't yet understand.

The rhythms, the sounds, the scintillation, the repetition, the surprise. The dream of the beat and the sound, organisms percolating under the pond, the creatures whose lives we can never grasp dancing upon the rhythms of plants we humans can never feel. We enumerate it, we transform it, we resonate it and make it play the drums and the bass.

Smack in the middle of last night, I suddenly woke up and just sat there staring awake at the dark ceiling. The wolf hour, absolute darkness, seemingly no sounds. There was nothing left to occupy my thoughts. There was nothing to worry about for the day ahead. My mind was absolutely blank. I thought back to the sounds of the pond, which by now always seem to matter.

Perfect Day

Here it is, in one picture, zoomed in for detail of the moment, the simple difference between plant and animal:

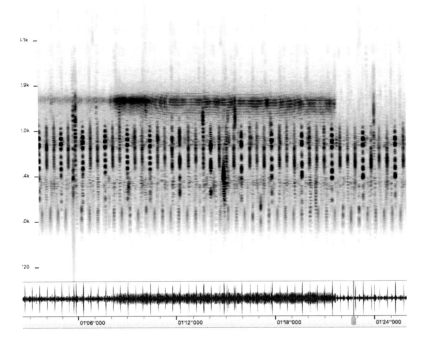

1:04–1:24, twenty seconds

We choose the scale at which we see images that tantalize us. The moiré of animal against the regular beat of plant.

For several years now I've been capturing these sounds, extracting their magic from the depths, taking them home and playing with them. But now I want to make music in the field, *right there*, live with the beating penises of the lesser water bugs, and the click click click of the photosynthetic vegetable beat.

Listening to their uneven beats I use that famous tendency of humans to hear patterns in everything. I might then add my own beat, at any tempo, hear how it gels. Maybe it will be a low *whoomp whoomp*, repeating for as long as it makes a groove that I don't get sick of, maybe a sample of a water boatman far slowed down, or a little thunk of a burbling brook.

I could play recognizable sounds or synthesizer ambiguities, remixing catbirds down to oscillators; all are possible tones for the moment, trying to enhance the mesmerizing percussion of the unknown water bugs. Occasionally a *conk-a-ree* of a red-winged blackbird joins in. Know that we are really out there, right next to the pond, making music out of the opportunity, finding beauty in the unfamiliar by resonating it together with affable tones.

There's a squeak from the pond. A bleep. A pond *kobold*, a lake monster, the *shake shake shake* of the boatmen. Their dick-waving comes and goes. I get cozy with the soundscape, and I find a way to play along.

Underneath Lost Pond by Jessica Jurassica

Inhabit the Pond
iPad performance recorded live along with the underwater creatures,
Hidden Lake, Fahnestock State Park, NY

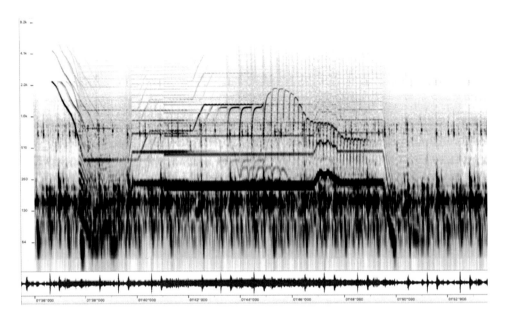

1:36-1:53, sixteen seconds

Midway in the journey of our second lockdown Spring I started performing live
with the pond, on iPad running electronic Animoog, Samplr, and Shoom
sounds, mixing the live underwater boatmen sounds with on-the-spot human
interaction.

I wanted a new way to play—no audience but the redwing blackbirds and me,
plus the submerged pond beasts who at times seemed to join in with what I was
doing.

Later when I listened to the underwater track I heard, not surprisingly, the low
bass sounds from the Bluetooth speaker coming from the iPad, which the insects could plainly hear. We know they respond to heavy vibrations, so why
wouldn't they do this underwater too? "Do the animals respond?" is the number one question people ask me when I make this interspecies music, and here
they seem to.

That question really doesn't interest me. I'm more interested in making a music no one species could make alone. It is unclear who this music is for—you, me, or the universe.

All are welcome.

What makes the *perfect day* by the pond?

In late spring, late May I walk out there. The trees are tinged with a luminous green. The forest sounds tropical as the orioles have arrived. Orioles! Why does no one study the song of this bird? Each one seems different, singing gentle, repeating melodies, exotic yet human. It is a warm sticky afternoon. No one else is out, as if they don't realize how beautiful the day is. It becomes a perfect day.

I record below and above, later mixing the two. I swear, those pond creatures seem to respond to the electronics I play. After some time, I can't tell who is making which sounds, the above and below are one. I am out of my element, no clarinets or other winds. All strange machines. Creatures too can sound like electronics. The technology, however alien, can still bring us closer.

A rhythm is a sound that repeats. On and on, the pop, the bubble, I've learned to think these things are more likely plant than animal. But sometimes we still cannot tell. Sometimes the water boatman still gets so loud who can imagine it could ever be so loud! They resound out of nowhere... I wonder how they are hearing what we hear. I want you to read all this while you listen to bring meaning to the swirl.

The method is simple: run the hydrophone under the water into a speaker above the water, so everyone can hear it: birds, frogs, terrestrial insects, deer, raccoons, squirrels. When *they* all hear the subaqueous sounds, they often respond, because it's not all that far from their world.

Any humans nearby, their ears perk up too.

Then I play live along with all the sounds around: sometimes on clarinet, more often on electronics: here I'm playing Samplr, Shoom, and a new app, GeoShred running the SWAM cello instrument. That technical info is in case you too want to try the same.

Once I came on stage after hearing Oswaldo Golijov's "Prayers for Isaac the Blind" played by Giora Feidman who could barely see himself. I was studying the sheet music. Feidman crept up behind me, and behind coke bottle glasses he said, "Ah, so you vant to know the secrets?"

I am revealing my secrets to you, telling you what software to use on an iPad. Still, I can't teach you how to listen to the results. You have to do that for yourself.

Above and Below
Live performance at the pond

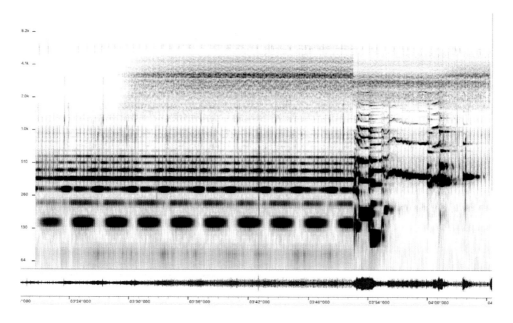

3:21-4:05, forty-four seconds

Look at that picture! The high repetitions are the water boatmen. Below are the *whoomping* electronicky emulated pondy sounds. On the right the celloesque melody appears. Real or unreal?

It is definitely live, out there by the pond, above and below the water, away from the virtual space at last.

Take me anywhere, anywhere, anywhere into *the world!* The opposite of what Baudelaire said.

It works. The more time I spend here the more each sound comes to mean something else. The world becomes alive, full of ideas. I want each click to move, each plop and fizz. Listeners wonder.

Lac de L'Aliette, Chamouille

Ilgin writes after listening to the depths.

> I've been inside and outside.
> Inside and outside, inside and outside
> Till I shed the skin of my tail.
> No one awaits their turn around here.
> No. 1, in their decent shape of one.
> But goblins, gas-beings, swaggering serpents, germ-mud,
> the coin-eyed gatekeeper, bridge-makers, belowroad-builders…
>
> Who can sound back at this.
> Who can talk back about this.
> Ask now,
> Now.
> As if solving a riddle,
> Find the treasure.

We set the times to listen to all our music. What we like, what we dislike. I know John Cage urged us to *free* ourselves from our likes and dislikes but without preferences what is it we got left? Do I like or dislike you? Does it matter? What matters is the work we can create together which cannot be done apart. The ease or unease of words meeting music. Stories about people the other of us does not know. Does it matter who each tale is about? You're so vain, I bet you think this song is about you. Don't you? I learned that line as a kid long before I had any idea why anyone would say such a thing. Now I know that if the song is good, you bet you should think it's about you. Why else would you sing along?

I wanted the songs of birds, whales, bugs, and wind to also be there for *me*. And now I am saying it about the mix of all deep down in the pond.

Like Robert Walser said in my epigraph with which we started, while he walked, he almost heard what no one would hear until centuries later: "…a soft, scarcely perceptible sound down there; he can hear it, but he can also see it. *That* is something new."

"Somewhere I read that music was invented to confirm human loneliness," writes poet Bessie Golding in the *New Yorker*. "But from the same source I learned that truth disappears in the telling of it."

I want music to bring us together, to say things that can be said no other way.

The proximity of other beings once again moves us. After all those years of virtual connection, time to meet in person.

I finally do meet Ilgin Deniz Akseloğlu in a French monastery in the middle of nowhere, a part of the country with few tourists, even in more open times. It is a residency for artists. Performers of all types. Even those who want to become performers are not sure how or what they will perform. Once a hundred nuns there, and then it became a school. Now it belongs to fifty artists, and no one is in charge.

You can say: I have a project, so let's go there and "make drama," as she first wrote. If it can't happen here then where can it happen?

It has already been happening, for more than a year, in that invisible place of the virtual world.

Some words, it is said, should only be spoken. *Others* should be written down. Here is how she prepared me:

Can we meet where everything stops?

That's the only place where I can hear myself. Found only when vanished, diffused in place. Between the field and here, there is an eternal gap. A canyon between the soul-call and body-memory.

I hear the cogwheels of the city outside. It is as if the gap is being squeezed constantly into a tube it cannot fit. It will have to explode in recurring intervals. The bleakness of today is partly having run out of the unexpected.

Is this distance an inspiration to feel the beauty of longing? To see how one can reach arms without extending. In the continuous waning and waxing, all the stories of a lifetime are packed in one letter of difference. In one single letter, I hear them though they are not here. I see them though I've never known them. I touch them as I feel other beings. This longing makes me a limb. The illusion of separation becomes an allusion of sufficiency—or whatever it may be.

You & I, what do we have in between?
An in-between that coats, envelops my being.
An in-between that is a search, a pursuit.
An in-between that is our correspondence.

The image of the edge stayed with me so long that I have no memory of any time before that. Edge has been the only line where expression was possible. Always in a rush, to go over Jesuit myths, edge has been my home, a home with blade-roots growing from the ground towards the ceiling. The more the blade-roots grew, the less I suffocated, the more I bled. A visceral journey home. One can only see in the dark. On the midway between the edge and the dark, it's dry and safe. Protected from a fall or a rise, in a cyclical routine. A resonating ladder is available, intermittently. A ladder like the double-headed serpent.

This point of rest, is home. There is no slipping away from here, unwittingly. It tells me, "Sweetheart, maybe, the edge is a curve. From where you shape as you reshape the gap. It's where the worlds meet."

Çizgi uzun
Çizgi uzun
Dur artık
Duy artık

Sonsuz boş
Sonsuz boşşşşş

Umarsız, umarsız gün

Menzil yok
Menzil yok

Ne varsa, duyanda
Ne varsa, duyduguanda

Köşe boş
Köşe boş

Gel eve gel
Ev sana gelecek.

[TRANSLATION:]

Line long
Line long
Stop now
Hear now

Void eternal
Void eternal

Remediless, remediless day

No distance
No distance

Only the one who heard is
Only that moment one heard is

Void edge
Void edge

Home, come home

It is not only the rumbling sounds under the surface of the pond, but all of our clicking and whistling codes of communication, be we dolphins, manatees, catbirds, or mice. So much is being said and rarely heard.

Here is the St Erme studio, an old nunnery that once held hundreds of nuns, now home to just a few artists, each at work on different performance projects assembled from all over the globe.

We wander the complex looking for microphones, stands, wires, holders, and assemble it all together thinking about all these creatures and their possible sounds. Atop the previous sonogram, high fragments of scratching creatures, each note sampled, musical material. In the middle, extended resonances, deep clarinets below.

They Keep Calling
St. Erme, France
David Rothenberg, keyboards, electronics, clarinet
Ilgin Deniz Akseloğlu, words and vocals

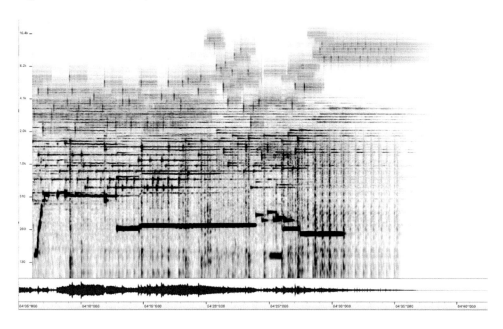

4:05-4:36, thirty-one seconds

Words improvised, singing all that we now remember:

> In heaven
> They keep calling from another time.
> From another day,
> They keep calling
>
> Go towards the temple
> High and roofless
> Roofless
>
> Ah..
> I...
> I don't know
> I don't know

How can one walk without feet?
How can one talk without mouth?
I don't know, don't know

I... I don't know
They touch the wall with my face.

The piano woozles, notes bend and extend. The creatures are played out of silence, the familiar is stretched toward the unknown.

The transformed sounds are thus both actual and imaginary at the same time. Data originally as sound is turned into other sounds. Like visualization, which you have seen throughout this book, there is also something called sonification, turning a different kind of data into sound.

Sonograms are visualizations of sound, to reveal structures that are easier for scientists to see than to hear. Sometimes the opposite method is tried, where data is turned into sound, so we can listen to patterns that otherwise wouldn't be noticed. There are kinds of rhythm whose value can be felt more readily than if we just look at them, or calculate their probability. You see, scientists also want to dance.

My resonating of pond beats into tones is also a kind of sonification. I want to make the ponds' actual sounds more alluring and more beautiful.

Here I go further, after realizing one can map the rhythmic aspect of any sound into a midi drum track, and chart the melodic aspect of any sound into a midi melody track. This is a way for the sound of the pond not only to be made more musicky, but for the sound to become a musician, to actually 'play' drums and bass, revealing rhythms that come from life in the water but perhaps things no human would care to notice or create. Let the pond be my muse, let the pond play my music, let the bass and drums from the pond be two-thirds of my trio.

Mendebur in Rain

Lac de L'Aliette recorded in pouring rain, Chamouille, France
Ilgin Deniz Akseloğlu, voice added after
contralto clarinet also from the studio, plus sonified drum'n'bass

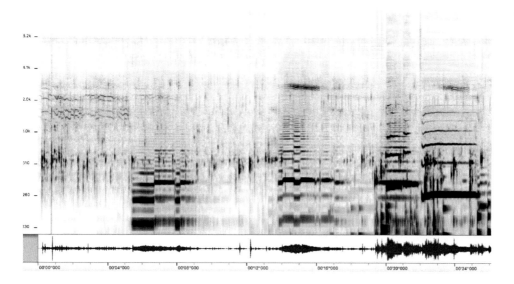

0:00–0:25, twenty-five seconds

This piece is a startling example of finding something where at first I thought there was nothing. This recording was so noisy, happening in the midst of a cloudburst thunderstorm, all our bags and equipment got soaked but everything still seemed to work.

Amazingly, beneath the rain was the strange whine of a bug. I would like to be able to identify this species for you but I still have no idea what it is. The crackling of water and weed was sonified into bass and drums. Then Ilgin explored the idea of some gargantuan monster howling undersea.

I added my favorite inscrutable superdeep sound, the big contralto clarinet that never leaves my studio. It may never fit into its case again.

Like Tom Waits sings, "there's a world going on, underground."

A troubled recording turns into something beautiful. And Ilgin Deniz knows how to add language to the pattering deep:

Gargantua
Leviathan
Mendebur
Typhon
Goliath
Behemoth
Homo Homini lupus!
Mo mo mo Monster
Putrefy putrefy…
Decay!
Perish perish..
Rot away …

As she later explains it:

Gargantua is a very massive, rapidly spinning black hole. It is orbited by the planets Miller and Mann as well as an unnamed neutron star. *Leviathan* is a creature with the form of a sea serpent in Judaism.

Mendebur is difficult to translate… here are some usages: drunken, swindler, smashing, disgusting, slovenly, bastard, son of a bitch… comes from Arabic, and also means "the one that comes from the West," but in Arabic culture,

West means 'from behind'—so, mendebur also means 'the one who betrays'—comes sneakily from behind and hurts.

Goliath is described in the biblical Book of Samuel as a Philistine giant defeated by the young David in single combat.

Music is fundamentally an in-person, in-nature game. Now I'm ready to travel the world finding others who can bring their voices into the sounds, bringing whatever perspectives they know.

Ilgin, Antti, Jérôme, Benjamin, Camille, David, all diving deep into the pond of mystery and desire.

I'd rather tell you that my obsession with the tiniest of underwater sounds has finally brought me to the whole meaning of life that I started out wanting to write about, forty years ago.

You'll have to be the judge of that if you have lasted this long in the story. For that alone I am eternally grateful. "What a privilege," Leonard Cohen used to say at the start of his concerts, "to be here together while the world is full of so much horror and strife." What an honor it is to tell all these stories to you, and to share what we have done with the sounds.

My aim is to fail to describe all this music so you will have no choice but to listen to it. Then you may decide if it's been worth all this trouble to make.

Impossible Happiness

When I was younger, maybe just starting out, I thought I knew everything, or if not quite that, then at least thought I possessed a grand new vision of the world, a picture of the whole that was unique and could genuinely teach people how to live. I sent it to writers, editors, publishers, and they tended to say the same thing: 'This is the kind of book you should write later in your life, when you've been around a bit longer, seen some things, lived and loved and traveled the world, worked hard to find a place solid enough to be ready to impart some wisdom for truly living. You're too young for that. Go out and find your place, explore, do something specific and real. Come back to me in forty years.'

Well, now it's been a few decades and I no longer feel tempted to give anyone any sort of advice. Or claim that one grand theory could rule them all. These days I want to investigate phenomena as tiny and intricate as possible—like the secret sounds of ponds.

We zoom in. We see images and find sounds that tantalize us. The moiré of creature against the regular beat of plant. Animal, vegetable, or mineral? The old game asks. The new game is a thousand questions, a million questions, the impossibility of any complete answer. One must be wary of finding order where none really exists. Human beings are seekers of patterns. We desperately want the world to mean something. And what if all these rhythms and tones are mere accidents of evolution?

I finally track down Jérôme Sueur after months of trying. These days he's busier than ever. Has a popular new radio show on the sounds of nature. He has been curating a grand exhibition for the Paris Philharmonie entitled *Musicanimale*.

So, I ask, have you had time to decode the myriad different creatures serenading deep down in the ponds surrounding the Musée de l'Histoire Naturelle, in Paris or anywhere near?

> No, as you know David, we have not really made all that much progress. Ask Camille. Too many creatures, too many sounds. Who knows who's making which ones? But my thinking on this situation has changed, these many years

later since you first contacted me. Maybe the individual sounds matter less than the whole. There is an ecology of sounds down there, under the surface. The whole health of the pond's biodiversity can be heard in one fell swoop, in the whole composition, the underwater symphony, or the sweep of the band.

Why should we consider each part to be more valuable than the whole? Go deep looking for one sound and you may find the meaning of all of them. *Everything sings, everything sounds*; it all swirls around us together. We can never get enough of seeing ourselves mirrored in our surroundings. This false identification turns out to be one of the reasons why it's so difficult to get people to accept behavior change to slow climate change.

Somewhat insulated from popular culture, scientists are trying to find ways to evaluate the ecological health of a pond, using various indexes (indices) to create a single number that evaluates the condition of the pond. There is an Acoustic Complexity Index that examines how busy and confusing the sounds appear. The Acoustic Diversity Index that measures how many kinds of sounds appear at once. There is an Acoustic Richness Index looking at how fluidly all the sounds fit together. And a Normalized Difference Soundscape Index that examines how much the continuous thrum of human noises might upset or invade the presence of everything else.

No scientist has yet proposed a Natural Musicality Index, but it just might be possible. We could measure how beautiful a pond might sound.

Jérôme Sueur laughed at me when I suggested this to him last week at *Musicanimale* in Paris. But I think we just might figure it out.

You may by now have noticed how insect numbers are declining. We no longer drive by summer fields finding our windshields covered in smushed bugs. Many surveys see insect numbers down by fifty percent or more, an ecological tragedy. The birds who eat them, writes Jay Griffiths, "are starving into the great silence." Musing upon this fact is the one thing that has led her to be at a loss for words:

> But what words do you suggest I use here? Annihilation? The end of worlds? The last generation? Absolute apocalypse? If you were looking this full in the face, what expresses it sufficiently? A savage anger overcomes me. This is not

a game. *Nature is not a hobby.* Protecting insects, children, and life is a necessary duty, incumbent on us all.

The singing presence of pond insects, even those dancing whirligig beetles that have graced many of my photos here, can be a sign of healthy, oxygenated water. We need pond life as much as the ponds do. Attending to their music is one small way to honor their tingling beauty.

Back home I am leading a walk of listeners to Swan Lake in Westchester's Rockefeller Preserve. The event has been advertised as 'family-friendly,' so I expect some children will be there. "When we listen to the pond," I tell the organizers, "it's possible that nothing will happen for an hour. But if we wait, we are often rewarded by sounds."

"Nah," they frown. "That won't work. Kids have no patience these days. You have to give them something right away."

"Well," I reply. "I can always fake it by playing something recorded in another pond. But I'd rather not do that."

"We'll see," they say.

Sure enough, there's a good crowd, thirty people or so, of many ages. I warn them at once, "we may have to wait to hear anything."

"Okay," motions one father to his son. "Let's get going."

"No, Dad," the kid glares. "he said we have to wait. So, we'll wait."

He wasn't the only one. Turns out the kids had plenty of patience. It was their parents who didn't want to listen.

And sure enough, those who waited were rewarded indeed. A strange and unexpected sound came right from beneath us, in the water among the reeds. One plant started releasing oxygen, invisible bubbles: loud, clear, solid rhythmic, and then, after a while, resonated.

The version I include here is at half speed. After a while the basic beat is resonated to reveal a tonality hiding within:

Lake Near, Humans Far
the rhythms emerge...

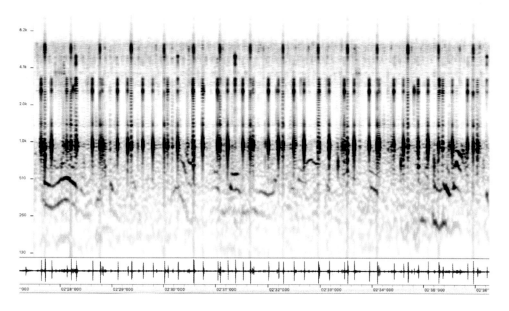

2:27-2:36, eleven seconds

In the background of this recording, high and faint, are the indistinct mumbles of terrestrial creatures: parents, children, others, chatting away.

But the pond plants, and occasional insects, are the louder rhythms here.

There are scientists who believe only humans can entrain to a beat, plus a few special songbirds like Snowball the cockatoo who dances to the Backstreet Boys. In my experience nearly all big parrots like to dance to a beat, and here, we've got an invisible plant who is doing it! What does this mean? Surely this is not an intentional music?

It is a found music, something going on all around us that usually remains unnoticed.

With this piece, we flip our experience into the background: This is the music of the pond heard from beneath the pond, the new world of sound we are now part of.

This is how the music ends, not with a whimper but a beat.

Once you hear them, you will not forget them. These pond musicians, animal and vegetable alike, are now part of our music, and there they'll remain.

Listen we all tell you. *Then listen again.* We wait, we hear, we wonder when to join in…

We want evidence. We toss the hydrophone in, and it gets covered in creatures, known and unknown.

We pack them up into a glass bowl to get really close to them, photographing them close up, and wondering what it is they're trying to say.

When it's time to let them go, a young boy named Leif says:

> There they go,
> back to their world of impossible happiness.

Show me the way and I'm there.

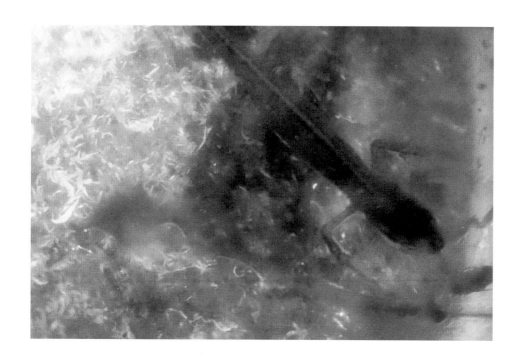

Cold Spring, NY

2020-2023

ACKNOWLEDGMENTS

Thanks to all those who have joined me on pond listening forays, that means Martina Decker, Julia Hill, Allison Hanes, Lindsay Stern, Marie Silkeberg, Sarah Connors, Emily Phillips, Nina Scibelli, Allison Cross, Umru Rothenberg, Paul Kahn, Dominique Negel, Etienne Turpin, Anna-Sophie Springer, Hanna Mattes, John Dubberstein, Lewis Rapkin, Tom Bregman, Sue Savage-Rumbaugh, Peter McConnell, Gabriella Magnani, Gustavo Valdivia, Claire Furtwangler, Lima Vafadar, David Michael, Andrea Lynn, Peter Kuper, Eckhard Kuchenbecker, Lasse-Marc Riek, Sha, Jessica Jurassica, Martyna Poznańska, Uygur Vural, Alex Nowitz, Anita Soukizy, and Mirjam Schaub.

Thanks to the online posse of pond listeners: David de la Haye, Tom Fisher aka Action Pyramid, and Jez Riley French. Thanks to hydrophone pioneer Zach Poff, and Chinese factory liaison and engineer Gejing Jiang. Thanks to Jonas Gruska, for his microphone wizardry. I'm sure he'll make far better hydrophones than I sometime soon.

Thanks to the scientific club of Jérôme Sueur, Camille Desjonquères, and Ben Gottesman for continuing to ask the right questions about what is going on in those ponds.

Thanks to my first readers John P. O'Grady and Edwin Frank.

Thanks to Ilgin Deniz Akseloğlu for finding such inspiring language in the ponds and discovering her own voice for these words.

Thanks to Jaanika Peerna for being there always, above and beneath the waters and ice of the world.

APPENDIX 1
Secret Songs of Ponds: Soundtrack

David Rothenberg
featuring Ilgin Deniz Akseloğlu

Whatever you may make of the story, these sounds over the past five years have inspired and been sculpted into quite a lot of music. With each piece I included a sonogram, that is, a somewhat artistic printout of frequency against time, to show the visual ethos of each piece.

The general trajectory is from purely wild and underwater to human and reflection abovewater, loosely in line with the encounters and stories referenced above in the text you just read. (I'm thinking here of the cryptic numeric code organizing chapters at the end of Italo Calvino's *Mr Palomar*.)

Here is one QR code linking to all the pieces on Soundcloud.

https://soundcloud.com/user-828525518/sets/the-secret-sounds-of-ponds

They are also available as a regular album under the name *Secret Songs of Ponds* on all the usual streaming services—a slightly different selection to keep things interesting.

Below is every piece with a separate link, in case you are reading this on a device and want to click to them all directly:

Secret Songs of Ponds

David Rothenberg featuring Ilgin Deniz Akseloğlu

https://on.soundcloud.com/iYWBu

Cape Cod Long Pond
https://on.soundcloud.com/pmySh

Very Rhythmic Pond
https://on.soundcloud.com/9aNoj

Hidden Lake Water Boatmen
https://on.soundcloud.com/mcP5F

Little Pond Beasts with Clarinet
https://on.soundcloud.com/g1aWM

Lost Pond Mystery
https://on.soundcloud.com/EH32w

Secret Sounds Detroit audio
https://on.soundcloud.com/zdg7z

Secret Sounds Detroit video
https://youtu.be/xGUGeFRsFn0

Awosting Dam Busy with Clarinets
https://on.soundcloud.com/VqAsL

Plant from Animal
https://on.soundcloud.com/BfoHU

Boston Corners Original Pond
https://on.soundcloud.com/6VBaz

When, the Sound
https://on.soundcloud.com/q65AD

Nerindi
https://on.soundcloud.com/24ypU

Undaunted New Lands
https://on.soundcloud.com/15BJB

How Distance Works
https://on.soundcloud.com/cM5Sn

State Forest Ring
https://on.soundcloud.com/PiLM8

Inhabit the Pond
https://on.soundcloud.com/Lw97c

Above and Below
https://on.soundcloud.com/tGXDL

They Keep Calling
https://on.soundcloud.com/pCHca

Mendebur in Rain
https://on.soundcloud.com/181ME

Lake Near, Humans Far
https://on.soundcloud.com/hDooY

Produced by David Rothenberg
All titles published by Mysterious Mountain Music (BMI)
©℗ 2023

APPENDIX 2
The Aquabeat Hydrophone

A pond hydrophone needs to be sensitive only to nearby sounds, noises just a meter or so away from the device. These things are pretty simple, basically contact mics like the kind you might stick with putty to a guitar surface, encased in plastidip to keep it waterproof....

An hour north from me, further upstate, is a wonderful place called Wave Farm, an arts residency for sound artists on a former farm. It contains an experimental radio station and a landscape full of unusual permanent installations. One of them is a USB drive inserted into an old oak tree, where you can offload your files for stern safekeeping. Another is a floating hydrophone in a mucky pond, designed by the Brooklyn sound artist Zach Poff, a master of DIY electronics, a homebrew tinkerer. When I first heard the sounds coming out of this thing, I was impressed.... The thing runs constantly, 24 hours a day, and is so sensitive it easily picks up the rumble of cars from half a mile away. Whereas my fine-tuned whale hydrophone picks up hardly any sound in these local ponds.

I had Zach make me ten hydrophones to hand out to a trial group of sonic adventurers aged eight to eighty to see whether they would get excited about listening to the strange sounds inside a pond. Turns out people are quite surprised and inspired by these sounds and at first don't believe such a sound could come from beneath the water. It gets them listening more carefully and then asking questions, like: *why* do our ponds sound so interesting, why the most interesting in spring and summer? And then, why doesn't everybody know about this?

I wanted more hydrophones—hundreds at least. Let everyone who wants one be able to listen and record! Need a lot of them cheap, where do I go? China of course.

Zach wanted no part of this, he said. "Come on man, people should build their own. I don't want to be part of the decline of American manufacturing." He's right in a way, of course. We still have to learn how to make things.

I have absolutely nothing against manufacturing in China. I have been teaching classes on globalization for years at my university, the New Jersey Institute of Technology. Manufacturing things in the country that best knows how to build electronics makes sense to me—cooperation brings the world closer together. Of course, I don't want any workers over there to be treated badly… and they must be fairly paid.

The China connection started many years ago when I needed an underwater speaker to play music live to whales. My colleagues in Helsinki, thousands of miles away, already in 2006 pointed out that there was a company in Hoboken that made inexpensive underwater speakers, while most competing products cost five or ten times more. "Looks like that place is pretty close to your office," they told me. "Why don't you pay them a visit" and so I did. Gejing Jiang graduated from Tsinghua University, Beijing, China, and previously worked as an engineer of the South China Sea Institute of Oceanography, the Chinese Academy of Sciences.

Since then, I have followed Gejing's product development closely and used many of his speakers in Hawaii, Russia, and the Pacific Northwest. So of course, when I needed a hydrophone I would go to him. "Ah," he said. "I happen to be in China right now. Let's see how I can help you…."

The hydrophones are being manufactured by Shenzhen Xinyatu Sound Electronics Co., Ltd. in Guangdong Province, China . Their major products are piezoelectric elements, and they have 140 employees. The Aquabeat is priced reasonably enough so many people can afford them. All you need to use it is a small audio recorder (TASCAM DR-05X or Zoom H1N for example) and headphones or a portable speaker to enjoy.

You can order your hydrophone here:

https://tinyurl.com/5etr26dc

APPENDIX 3
A Short Guide to Pond Music

There are a handful of fine musicians out there also working with underwater pond sounds. The following releases are all available on Bandcamp:

David Dunn, *Angels and Insects*
Jana Winderen, *The Listener*
Leah Barclay *Subterranean Sketch*
David de la Haye, *Hidden Sounds (Underwater ASMR Edition)*
Action Pyramid, *Singing Below the Surface*
Slavek Kwi and David Michael, *Mmabolela*
Bernhard Wöstheinrich, *Submerging in a Forgotten Pond*
David Rothenberg, *Longform*

Annea Lockwood has been a great inspiration and a pioneer in watery recording and composition, especially known for her recordings of the Danube and Hudson rivers. There is a wonderful short film about her by Sam Green entitled *A Film About Listening* which can be found here: https://vimeo.com/ondemand/annealockwood

One of the great recent pond recordists was the late Tom Lawrence, who made the fabulous recording *Water Beetles of Pollardstown Fen*, released on the German label Gruenrekorder, known for its commitment to field recording:
https://www.gruenrekorder.de/?page_id=5235

Jan Hamrsky's website has invaluable advice on how to photography these underwater sonic beasts, www.lifeinfreshwater.net

SOME RELEVANT BOOKS

Ally, Matthew, *Ecology and Existence: Bringing Sartre to the Water's Edge*, Lanham: Lexington Books, 2017.
Blass, Tom, *Swamp Songs: Journeys Through Marsh and Meadow*, London: Bloomsbury, 2022.
Del-Claro, Kleber and Rhainer Guillermo, *Aquatic Insects: Behavior and Ecology*, Cham: Springer Nature Switzerland, 2019.
Evans, Paul, *Field Notes from the Edge: Journeys Through Britain's Secret Wilderness*, London: Rider Books, 2015.

Fischer, Norman, *Nature*, Berkeley: Tuumba Press, 2021.

Gagliano, Monica, *Thus Spoke the Plant*, Berkeley: North Atlantic Books, 2018.

Griffiths, Jay, *Why Rebel?* London: Penguin, 2021.

Hamrsky, Jan, *Freshwater Life*, Prague: Blurb, 2015.
   https://www.blurb.com/b/6306045-freshwater-life

Heckman, Charles, *Ecological Strategies of Aquatic Insects*, Boca Raton: CRC Press, 2018.

Hurd, Barbara, *Stirring the Mud: On Swamps, Bogs, and Human Imagination*, Athens:
   University of Georgia Press, 2001.

Kolbert, Elizabeth, *Under a White Sky: The Nature of the Future*, New York: Crown, 2021.

Lewis-Stempel, John, *Still Water: The Deep Life of the Pond*, New York: Doubleday, 2019.

Lispector, Clarice, *Agua Viva*, trans. Stefan Tobler, New York: New Directions, 2012.

Lodgson, Gene, *The Pond Lovers*, Athens: University of Georgia Press, 2003.

Mann, Michael, *The New Climate War: The Fight to Take Back Our Planet*,
   New York: Public Affairs, 2021.

Marks, Brady and Mark Timmings, *The Wetland Project: Explorations in Sound,
   Ecology, and Post-Geographical Art*, Vancouver: Figure 1 Publishing, 2022.
   [book features many QR codes with links to sounds, www.wetlandproject.com]

Moore, Kathleen Dean, *Earth's Wild Music: Celebrating and Defending the Songs of the
   Natural World*, Berkeley: Counterpoint, 2021.

Oram, Daphne, *An Individual Note of Music, Sound and Electronics*, London:
   Anomie, 2016 [1972].

Proulx, Annie, *Fen, Bog and Swamp: A Short History of Peatland Destruction and Its
   Role in the Climate Crisis*, New York: Scribner, 2022.

Rothenberg, David, *The Book of Music and Nature*, Middletown: Wesleyan Press, 2001.

Rothenberg, David, *Bug Music*, New York: St. Martins, 2013.

Rothenberg, David, *Nightingales in Berlin*, Chicago: University of Chicago Press, 2019.

Sherry, James, *Selfie: Poetry, Social Change & Ecological Connection*, New York: Palgrave
   Macmillan, 2022.

Sjöberg, Fredrik, *The Fly Trap*, trans. Thomas Teal, New York: Pantheon, 2015.

Strauss, Gerhard and Rolf Niedringhaus, *Die Wasserwanzen Deutschlands*,
   Osnabrück: WABV, 2014.

Sudnow, David, *Talk's Body*, New York: Penguin, 1980.

Sueur, Jérôme, *Histoire naturelle du silence*, Arles: Actes Sud, 2023.

Sueur, Jérôme, *Le son de la Terre*, Arles: Actes Sud, 2022.

Tammsaare, A.H., *Vargamäe : Volume 1 of Truth and Justice*, Glasgow:
   Vagabond Voices, 2019.

Thorp, James and Christopher Rogers, *Field Guide to Freshwater Invertebrates of North
   America*, San Diego: Academic Press, 2011.

Urbonas, Nomeda and Gedmias Urbonas, eds. *Swamps and the New Imagination: On
   the Future of Cohabitation* London: Sternberg Press, 2024.

SELECTED SCIENTIFIC ARTICLES AND THESES

Abrahams C, Desjonquères C, Greenhalgh J. "Pond Acoustic Sampling Scheme: A draft protocol for rapid acoustic data collection in small waterbodies." *Ecology and Evolution*, 11, 2021, pp. 7532–7543. https://doi.org/10.1002/ece3.7585

Alcocer I, Lima H, Sugai L, Lluisa D, "Acoustic indices as proxies for biodiversity: a meta-analysis," *Biological Reviews* 97, 2020, pp. 2209–2236. https://doi.org/10.1111/brv.12890

Barratt EL, Davis NJ. "Autonomous Sensory Meridian Response (ASMR): a flow-like mental state. *PeerJ* 3, 2015. https://doi.org/10.7717/peerj.851

Desjonquères C, Gifford T, Linke S. "Passive acoustic monitoring as a potential tool to survey animal and ecosystem processes in freshwater environments." *Freshwater Biology*. 65, 2020, pp. 7–19. https://doi.org/10.1111/fwb.13356

Desjonquères C, Rybak F, Ulloa JS, Kempf A, Hen AB, Sueur J. "Monitoring the acoustic activity of an aquatic insect population in relation to temperature, vegetation and noise." *Freshwater Biol.* 2018, pp. 1–10. https://doi.org/10.1111/fwb.13171

Desjonquères C, Rybak F, Depraetere M, Gasc A, Le Viol I, Pavoine S, Sueur J. "First description of underwater acoustic diversity in three temperate ponds," *PeerJ*, 2015, https://doi.org/10.7717/peerj.1393

Desjonquères C, *Acoustic diversity and ecology of freshwater environments: Exploration in temperate environments* , Paris : Museum national d'histoire naturelle, 2016. https://desjonqu.github.io/assets/img/CDesjonqueres_These.pdf

Francomano D, Gottesman BL, Pijanowski B, "Biogeographical and analytical implications of temporal variability in geographically diverse soundscapes," *Ecological Indicators* 121, 2021, https://doi.org/10.1016/j.ecolind.2020.106794

Gottesman BL, Francomano D, Zhao Z, et al. "Acoustic monitoring reveals diversity and surprising dynamics in tropical freshwater soundscapes." *Freshwater Biology*, 2018, pp. 1–16. https://doi.org/10.1111/fwb.13096

Greenhalgh JA, Genner MJ, Jones G, Desjonquères C. "The role of freshwater bioacoustics in ecological research." *WIREs Water* 7, 2020. https://doi.org/10.1002/wat2.1416

Jansson A, "Audiospectrographic analysis of stridulatory signals of some North American Corixidae," *Annales Zoologici Fenneci*, 13, 1976, pp. 48-62.

Jansson A, "New records of Corixidae (Heteroptera) from northeastern USA and eastern Canada, with one new synonymy," *Entomologica Fennica* vol. 13, no. 2, 2022, pp. 85-88. https://doi.org/10.33338/ef.84140

Jansson A, *Stridulation and its significance in the waterbug genus* Cenocorixa, Vancouver: University of British Columbia, 1971. https://open.library.ubc.ca/soa/cIRcle/collections/ubctheses/831/items/1.0101890

Kratochvil HG, Pollirer M. "Acoustic effects during photosynthesis of aquatic plants enable new research opportunities." *Scientific Reports* 7, 2017. https://doi.org/10.1038/srep44526

Krause B, Farina A, "Using ecoacoustic methods to survey the impacts of climate change on biodiversity," *Biological Conservation* 195, 2016, pp. 245-254. https://doi.org/10.1016/j.biocon.2016.01.013

Linke S, Gifford T, Desjonquères C et al, "Freshwater ecoacoustics as a tool for continuous ecosystem monitoring," *Frontiers in Ecology and the Environment*, 2018, https://doi.org/10.1002/fee.1779

Onzik K, Gagliano M. "Feeling Around for the Apparatus: A Radicley Empirical Plant Science." *Catalyst: Feminism, Theory, Technoscience* 8 (1), 2022, pp. 1–19.

Poerio GL, Blakey E, Hostler TJ, Veltri T "More than a feeling: Autonomous sensory meridian response (ASMR) is characterized by reliable changes in affect and physiology." *PLoS ONE* 13 (6), 2018, https://doi.org/10.1371/journal.pone.0196645

Reid A, Hardie DJW, Mackie D, Jackson JC, Windmill JFC, "Extreme call amplitude from near-field acoustic wave coupling in the stridulating water insect *Micronecta scholtzi*." *Journal of the Royal Society Interface* 15, 2018. http://dx.doi.org/10.1098/rsif.2017.0768

Rountree RA, Juanes F, Bolgan M, "Temperate freshwater soundscapes: A cacophony of undescribed biological sounds now threatened by anthropogenic noise," *PLoS ONE* 15(3), 2020. https://doi.org/10.1371/journal. pone.0221842

Sueur J, Mackie D, Windmill JFC, "So Small, So Loud: Extremely High Sound Pressure Level from a Pygmy Aquatic Insect (Corixidae, Micronectinae)." *PLoS ONE* 6(6), 2011. https://doi.org/10.1371/journal.pone.0021089

van der Lee GH, Desjonquères C, Sueur J, Kraak M, Verdonschot P, "Freshwater ecoacoustics: Listening to the ecological status of multi-stressed lowland waters," *Ecological Indicators* 113, 2020. https://doi.org/10.1016/j.ecolind.2020.106252

Musician and philosopher **David Rothenberg** wrote *Why Birds Sing*, *Bug Music*, *Survival of the Beautiful*, *Nightingales in Berlin* and many other books, published in at least eleven languages. His two previous books of poetry are *Blue Cliff Record: Zen Echoes* and *Invisible Mountains*. His latest book is *Whale Music*. He has more than forty recordings out, including *One Dark Night I Left My Silent House* with Marilyn Crispell on ECM, and most recently *In the Wake of Memories* and *Faultlines*. He has performed or recorded with Pauline Oliveros, Peter Gabriel, Ray Phiri, Suzanne Vega, Scanner, Elliott Sharp, Iva Bittová, and the Karnataka College of Percussion. Rothenberg is a Distinguished Professor at the New Jersey Institute of Technology.

ROOF BOOKS

the best in language since 1976

Recent & Selected Titles

- FOR TRAPPED THINGS by Brian Kim Stefans, 138 pp. $20
- EXCURSIVE by Elizabeth Robinson, 140 pp. $20
- I, BOOMBOX by Robert Glück, 194 pp. $20
- TRUE ACCOUNT OF TALKING TO THE 7 IN SUNNYSIDE
  by Paolo Javier, 192 pp. $20
- THE NIGHT BEFORE THE DAY ON WHICH
  by Jean Day, 118 pp. $20
- MINE ECLOGUE by Jacob Kahn, 104 pp. $20
- SCISSORWORK by Uche Nduka, 150 pp. $20
- THIEF OF HEARTS by Maxwell Owen Clark, 116 pp. $20
- DOG DAY ECONOMY by Ted Rees, 138 pp. $20
- THE NERVE EPISTLE by Sarah Riggs, 110 pp. $20
- QUANUNDRUM: [i will be your many angled thing]
  by Edwin Torres, 128 pp. $20
- FETAL POSITION by Holly Melgard, 110 pp. $20
- DEATH & DISASTER SERIES by Lonely Christopher, 192 pp. $20
- THE COMBUSTION CYCLE by Will Alexander, 614 pp. $25
- URBAN POETRY FROM CHINA editors Huang Fan and
  James Sherry, translation editor Daniel Tay, 412 pp. $25
- BIONIC COMMUNALITY by Brenda Iijima, 150 pp. $20
- QUEENZENGLISH.MP3: POETRY: POETRY, PHILOSOPHY,
  PERFORMATIVITY, Edited by Kyoo Lee, 176 pp. $20
- UNSOLVED MYSTERIES by Marie Buck, 96 pp. $18.95

Roof Books are distributed by
SMALL PRESS DISTRIBUTION
1341 Seventh Street • Berkeley, CA. 94710-1403.
spdbooks.org

Roof Books are published by **Segue Foundation**
300 Bowery #2 • New York, NY 10012
seguefoundation.com

Made in the USA
Monee, IL
30 June 2024